HEART   D

God Bless.
I'm praying for you & yours

Saul

HEART OF A HUSBAND

DISCOVER WHAT IT MEANS TO LOVE YOUR WIFE AS CHRIST LOVES THE CHURCH.

PAUL HARRIS

Heart of a Husband
© Copyright 2019
Paul Harris

Edited by: R. Gene Crawford
Cover design by: Nathan Williams
Proofread by: Ike Jones
Chief Design Consultant: Andy Whaley
Art Director/Creative Consultant: Scott Kirby
Photography by: Sarah Bottarel Photography
Design Consultant: Jeremy Wells

Printed in The United States of America.

THANKS

As I consider the process of writing this book, there are so many people who have played a role in this journey. I am thankful for every word of encouragement and every prayer offered on my behalf over the past eleven years.

CINDY—my beautiful wife. You have always been God's promise to me. No matter how many times I have tried to mess it up, you have been there to offer me grace and mercy. You are my rock. I know you don't fully know all the strength and wisdom you have; you are the anchor of our family. I'm so thankful for you. I love you.

EMILY AND PAYTON—my incredible children. I'm inspired by you. I love getting to be your dad. I love your past and look forward to your future. I love my time with you. You are both becoming people I look forward to being friends with when you're grown. Keep being you. It doesn't matter what anyone else thinks. God made you to be you, and I love that person.

MY EXTENDED FAMILY—all of you, my beautifully blended family. As my grandma would say, "I'm thankful for the in-laws and the out-laws." You have extended me grace in my worst moments and have always encouraged me to be my best. Thanks, Mom and Dad, for always seeing who God said I was and always encouraging me to be just that. A special thanks to my stepparents and in-laws; you have always treated me like I was yours. I love you all.

HEART OF A HUSBAND GROUP—Though there are a bunch of names I could mention, I want to specifically mention this group of guys: Andy, Alan, Darin, Ike, Jeff, Jeremy, and Paul. You guys were willing to be guinea pigs in the *Heart of a Husband* project. Thank you for helping me create an atmosphere where it was okay for men to be vulnerable.

HOPE CHURCH—Whether pastors, staff, or members, you all have played an instrumental role in who I have become over the past twelve years. God brought my family to you only months before the lowest time of our lives. The role you played in our healing is so significant that I'm not sure I can even articulate it. I love this body. I love this family. I'm so happy to be part of what God is doing there.

MATT WOOD—You were the first person to read manuscripts in my early days of writing. You weren't even married yet, but you always encouraged me. Thank you for being there in the beginning and telling me that I was on the right path, even though I wasn't sure at times.

ANDY BRODRICK—God put you in my life right on time. You are my "author friend." You read the book as I wrote it. You gave input and encouragement. You are wise. You are smart. You are kind. You are a great representative of Heaven. Thank you for who you are in my life.

PAUL WINDISCH—God has given me a great friend in you. When I met you seven years ago, I could never have predicted who you would have become in my life. You have been my cheerleader, my encourager, and my friend. Thank you for so many words of encouragement. I'm thankful for our "fire dances." I'm thankful to get to grow in the Lord with you. I'm thankful that God placed you in my life.

FREEMDOMHOUSE—Wow guys! I love the way God works. It's been eleven years since that last service at Landmark Church. Yet over the years, we have stayed connected. I love how God brings everything full circle. Here we are eleven years later, and you are playing a role in the publication of this book. I love you. I love the role you played in me better understanding my call and purpose. Gene, Ike, Kirby, Mark—Thank you.

CONTENTS

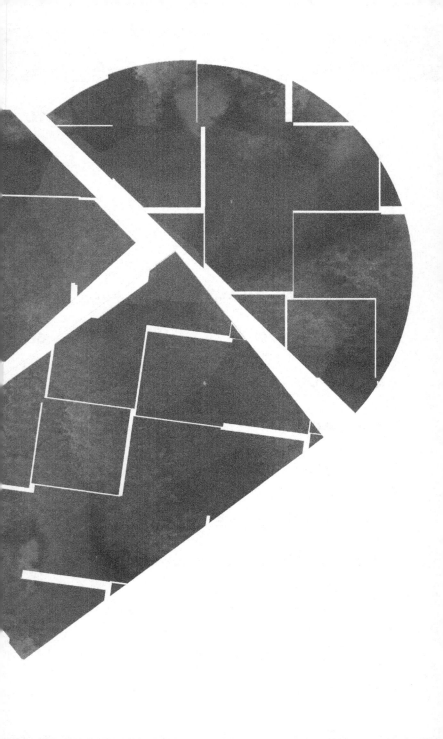

HUSBANDS,
LOVE YOUR WIVES,
AS CHRIST LOVED THE CHURCH AND GAVE HIMSELF UP FOR HER.

Ephesians 5:25

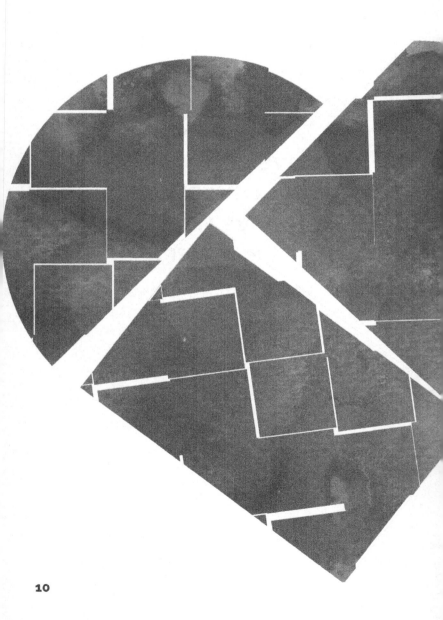

I f you're reading this book, then you're likely married, plan to be married, or hope to gain insight on how not to lose another marriage. Regardless of where you are on your journey, I'm confident that you're ready to glean some knowledge on how to be a good or better husband.

I won't pretend that I'm some kind of expert who will give you the secret recipe to become a perfect husband that will make your wife always feel like a queen; I fail at this daily. Instead, I will expose my life and share with you the experiences and revelations that I've had over the past few years regarding being a husband—specifically, a husband that strives to love his wife as Jesus loves His Bride, the Church.

If you are or have been married, you know that it's a journey of ups and downs. (And if you aren't yet, you'll learn soon enough.) There are mountain peaks and valleys. Navigating that up-and-down journey is the challenge we have before us. How will you choose to navigate that journey of marriage? I can tell you that before I wrote this book, I would have said that I was a pretty good husband. I told my wife that she was pretty. I bought her gifts. I affirmed her in what she did or attempted to do. But when I was confronted with the truth of God's idea of what a husband is, I immediately felt challenged. I learned that unless you want to know the answers, don't ask. But if you really want to know what it looks like to be the kind of husband you were intended to be, keep reading.

I believe with all my heart that we are called to be more than we realize when it comes to being great husbands. It's more than showing up for just the significant events. It's more than compliments and flowers. Being a husband is a lifestyle—a lifestyle of sacrifice, loss of self, and gain of unity that looks like

Jesus and His Church, His Body, His Bride.

In this book, you won't find a bullet list of the secrets of a great marriage. Instead, this text holds something I believe to be much deeper than that. I believe it contains the truth about the relationship that God intended for us with Him and with our wives.

As you read, I pray that God reveals himself and His intentions for you to you. I pray that as you work through the following pages, you will approach them with a soft heart. I'm guessing that you wouldn't even be reading this book if you didn't at least have good intentions about being a better husband. I don't know how good or how bad you perceive your marriage to be, but I pray that as you read, God will empower you to listen and obey what He says about being a husband. I pray that we all learn to love our wives just like Jesus loves the Church, and in the process, understand the true heart of a husband.

CHAPTER ONE

WHY ME?

WHY AM I WRITING
A BOOK ABOUT MARRIAGE?

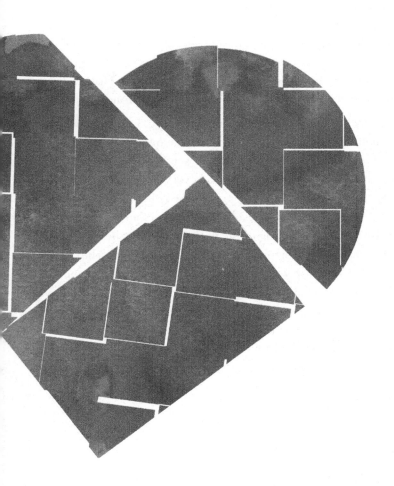

When a wise man is instructed, he gains knowledge.

Proverbs 21:11

So, why me? Why am I writing a book on marriage? I'm afraid that once I explain why I'm writing the book, you may find me even less qualified. I'm writing on this topic because I did almost everything I could to ruin mine. That's right; I'm going to tell you how to save your marriage by explaining how I almost lost mine. It seems almost hypocritical unless you look at it from the perspective of someone who has been to hell and back and is now here to help you steer clear of that path. That's definitely how I would describe it: I have been to hell and back.

It all happened a little over ten years ago. I was married to my high school sweetheart, Cindy, a little over six years. Our daughter was four years old, and our son was almost one. From the outside, it appeared that we had everything anyone could want. But like many marriages, we were going through the motions. At the time, I was traveling with a worship band and living my dreams. I was making music with some of my best friends, and we had the opportunity to lead thousands in worship. I allowed that ministry to become the most important thing in my life. Though it wasn't conscious at the time, constantly being away from the family to minister had become justifiable in my mind. Things had gotten to the point that Cindy and I couldn't get along because I was so busy with my job, the church, and the band. She constantly felt alone. Meanwhile, I perceived her complaining about me being gone so often as her not being supportive.

I'll never forget the day that I gave up. I was on my way out the door to the last of four out of seven days on the road. Cindy was dealing with a colicky baby, and she had nearly enough of my continual absence. I was so consumed with what I was doing that I never stopped to think about how it might be affecting my family. I believed that I was doing God's will, and nothing was going to get in the way of that—not even my family. The van arrived to pick me up. The baby was crying, I was leaving, Cindy was not happy, and we exchanged harsh words. This is a moment that I still have etched in my mind. I remember feeling something crack. There was now a divide, and I was no longer interested in making anything work between the two of us.

I urge you to never become so consumed with yourself and where you think God is leading that you aren't willing to make adjustments to save your marriage. I once heard someone say, "Your 'no' needs to be as loud as your 'yes.'" I wish I had heard that before it was too late. There were certain things in my life at that time I really needed to say no to, loudly.

After I decided that our marriage couldn't, or wouldn't, be saved, I was an open target for what soon would prove to be an attack from the enemy. That assault would knock down everything I had built on what proved to be a shaky foundation. Of course, a lot of my revelation comes from looking back on what I've been through. As the old saying goes, "hindsight is 20/20."

A few months before I felt the crack, I began developing a friendship with another woman. Honestly, when we started our friendship, it was innocent. I would never have dreamed that I would wind up in a relationship with any woman other than my wife. I've always been a friendly person and had plenty of women as friends. It had never been an issue for me. I didn't feel like I had anything to guard against on that front. I realize now that as a man, especially a husband, you always have to be on guard.

Now, listen to the way the enemy deceived me. At the same time I began feeling that my wife wasn't supporting me and things were at an end, I started to get support from someone else. I never really made the connection then. I was too busy enjoying hearing someone tell me that I was wise, I was smart, and I was perfect. The problem was that I relied on that praise as the kind of emotional support that should only come from a wife. I allowed myself to become a clean canvas for the other woman in my life to paint how I perceived myself.

It had been about a month since the day I gave up on my marriage, and I found myself in a relationship with a woman that was not my wife. Over the next five months, I lived a secret life that brought me to the brink of losing everything that I had.

Eventually, I told Cindy about what I was doing. I expected that she would give me what I deserved and kick me out on my butt. But through a broken voice and tear-filled eyes, she asked me to stay. I'll never forget how broken her voice was. I'll always remember how her face was so filled with pain. I had caused this. My selfishness and lack of concern for my wife had led us to this moment.

At that moment, the woman I had forsaken and rejected chose to forgive me. At that moment, Cindy truly modeled Jesus to me. Though she had every justifiable reason to leave me, she offered mercy and grace. We spent the next few days trying to figure out how we got to this place. Then about four days after I told her about the affair, I felt the crack that had developed only seven months before seal up. I can still remember where I was standing when the healing started. I came home from work and found Cindy on the floor, crying as she watched our wedding video. I immediately came face to face with everything I had done. I could see the pain that I had caused all over her face. At that very moment, I felt the division that existed in me come together as the crack closed. It swallowed up every feeling I had for the other woman. Thank you, Jesus!

After realizing that Cindy was serious about staying with me, and with my heart no longer divided, I began to ask God, "Where in the Bible does it teach me to be a good husband?" I then remembered the scripture where husbands are instructed to love their wives like Jesus loved the church. Was this the answer to my question? Do I love my wife like Christ loves the church? I hustled over to Ephesians chapter five to find more instruction in the chapter that holds that verse, but that was kind of it. There were no super instructions on how to do it. It was simply, "Husbands, love your wives, as Christ loved the church and gave himself up for her" (Ephesians 5:25).

I began to pray and ask the Lord, "What does that mean?" This book is a collection of what was revealed to me over time. I have found that Jesus takes His relationship with us very seriously. Honestly, it's why we exist—to be in relationship with Him.

That explains "Why Me?" as an author, but you may be wondering "Why Me?" as a reader. I know that the odds are that you haven't cheated on your wife by having a physical affair. Yet one reason you may need this book is that maybe you're tempted to be unfaithful. Another reason may be that you're unaware that there are areas of unfaithfulness beyond that physical act. Two of the most significant areas are pornography and emotional affairs. Many men, in my experience, find these two traps to be innocent and not something to be concerned with. But that couldn't be further from the truth!

Be cautious about allowing close relationships and emotionally deep conversations with women other than your wife. If you're sharing your deepest feelings or confiding in a woman who isn't in your family or your wife, stop! Emotional affairs are the trailhead to a path that leads to pain and sorrow. It's easy for men to want to be affirmed by others, but there's a level of affirmation that should only come from the woman you've committed to be with the rest of your life.

Consider the way you interact with women who aren't your wife or a family member. I've found that many things I previously thought were just being friendly can be easily misinterpreted as flirting, or even worse, an interest in intimacy. Recently at a restaurant with my wife, she brought to my attention this kind of inadvertent behavior. I have a genuine love for people, so I often make conversation with my server. I honestly don't think much of it. As I asked for a refill, I reached up and touched the server's elbow and said, "thank you" as she walked away. My wife kindly asked me, "Do you always touch the servers when you ask for something?" Cindy wasn't mad at me. She was asking me with a sarcastic sweetness—but I got her point. What was innocent to me, could have been seen as something more, especially if I had been to dinner by myself. It's essential, as men, to always be aware of the impression we're leaving on the other gender.

While studies show that only 20% of men have reported having sex with someone other than their wives while married, the percentage increases significantly once you consider those who view pornography. Some studies show that as much as 60% of Christian men have admitted that they look at pornography. Jesus' words in Matthew 5:27–28 have something to say about this: "You have heard that it was said, 'You shall not commit adultery.' But I say to you that everyone who looks at a woman with lustful intent has already committed adultery with her in his heart."

I want to say this next part in the most loving and non-judgmental way possible. But I feel it's necessary to let you know that if you're looking at pornography, you are cheating on your wife. You need to confess your sin to her and God to start on the road to healing. Thankfully, porn has never been a temptation for me, but I have friends who have struggled with it. I've seen them confess this to their wives, and I can assure you that the recovery is still a road of rebuilding trust and security. I pray that if this is your struggle, you find the strength to sit down with your wife and confess so that you can have the marriage that God intended for you. There is a Scripture that kind of sums this up. In John 8:31–32, Jesus encourages us to stay faithful to His teachings. If we do this, we'll know the truth, and it will set us free. In this case, I can assure you that the truth will set you free and set you on the path of healing. Bringing His truth into your relationship is the only way to experience proper freedom. Confessing to your wife isn't going to be easy, but it is the way to getting your relationship back on track.

You may have noticed that I mentioned that my failure happened a little over ten years ago, yet I felt the urge to write this book over eleven years ago. If I had written this book at that first urge, the part you're reading right now would be very different. But as I write this now, I intend to use the tragedy I endured to encourage you to avoid the snares that caught me. I would have much rather averted that tragedy, but having endured it, I pray that my story will help you avoid such a place in your life. God truly can take what was intended for evil and make something good. I pray that He encourages you as you read this book. But most of all, I pray you are inspired to obey God and His Word. That is the most powerful step you can take to affect your marriage positively. Whether it is through reading the Bible, through another sharing His Word, or just God's still, small voice speaking to you—listen and obey.

ASK YOURSELF

1. Is there a crack in my marriage due to unfaithfulness? If there is, no matter how big or small, you need to confess. Truth can set your marriage free if you're vulnerable and honest. I realize that not every story may end up like mine, but your soul can't experience real freedom if you're living in a lie.

2. Am I currently having an emotional affair? You may have never considered doing this, but you should assess every relationship you have with someone of the opposite sex. Look at the emotional reliance you have on that person compared to your spouses.

3. Do I need to confess anything to my wife? If you do, pick a safe place for your wife to do this. She needs to be free to react however she needs. I would also recommend that you choose a safe place for you (no knives, frying pans, or blunt objects).

4. Am I committed to the relationship God has intended for me and my wife? Will I commit to doing anything and everything I can to save my marriage?

LET'S PRAY

Heavenly Father, thank You for new revelations. As we pursue Your heart for our marriage, we pray for wisdom, knowledge, and understanding. We ask for a soft and open heart to acknowledge where we can improve when it comes to loving our wives. Thank You for Your wonderful example of being a great husband. Please help us to live and love like You. Teach us to be like You. We commit before You to give up our will for Yours. Help me to love my wife like You love the Church. In Jesus' name, amen.

THOUGHTS & REFLECTIONS

CHAPTER TWO

GIVE IT UP

LETTING GO OF OUR WILL CAN BE A SCARY THING.

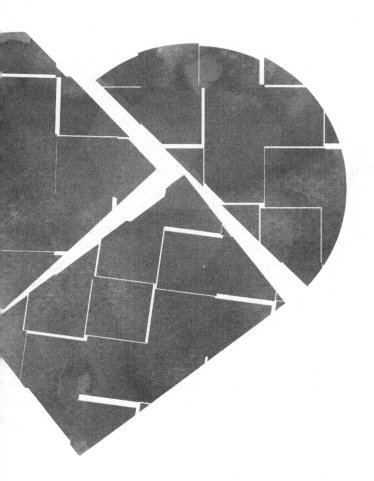

Then Jesus went with them to a place called Geth-semane, and he said to his disciples, "Sit here, while I go over there and pray." And taking with him Peter and the two sons of Zebedee, he began to be sorrow-ful and troubled. Then he said to them, "My soul is very sorrowful, even to death; remain here, and watch with me." And going a little farther he fell on his face and prayed, saying, "My Father, if it be possible, let this cup pass from me; nevertheless, not as I will, but as you will."

Matthew 26:36–39

As I begin to consider this chapter, I find myself in kind of a spiritual depression. (I think that's the right diag-nosis.) I know that God is with me and that God loves me in spite of me, but I feel down—sad almost. I find myself wondering what the catalyst for this funk is. Am I tired? Over-worked? Bored? Or could it be something different? Could it be my spirit knows the heaviness that comes with writing this chapter? It's a scary title: Give It Up. I'm considering one of the ways that Jesus loves the Church, and thereby one of the ways I'm to love my wife. Ultimately, giving up one's will is a scary proposition.

I wonder how scared Jesus was that night in the Garden of Gethsemane. We get a little insight into His mind. He went to the Garden with His closest followers. He then went a little farther to pray. As He began to pray, He begged the Father to allow the soon-coming cup of suffering to pass Him. The cup was His death, the cup of our deliverance. He then quickly followed up with those famous words, "nevertheless, not as I will, but as you will" (Matthew 26:39). At that moment, we probably get the closest look at Jesus' human nature. He knew the purpose He was committed to from birth, but at this moment, He hoped for another way out. He knew what the Father sent Him for, but when it came down to it, the fully human Jesus hoped that there was another way out. While His friends slept, even though He had asked them to pray, He made the most significant decision of His life. After some prayer time in the Garden, Jesus knew what He would do because of His great love for His Bride, the Church. He would give up His will.

As men, we have it bred in us to win. We don't give up; we take over. Our society teaches us to do all that we can to win. Giving up is never on any top ten lists of how to succeed. I'm a firstborn son. I was the firstborn grandchild. In almost everything I've been involved in, I became the one in charge. I guess I would say that giving up my will isn't something that comes easily or naturally for me. I like things the way I like them. I want things the way I want them, and I consider myself pretty good at convincing others that's what is best. So, as I prayed to God for ways to understand how to love my wife better and pursued understanding of exactly how he loves the Church, I got a little nervous when he so sweetly responded, "I gave up my will for you. That's one of the ways I loved you." Okay, so here I was, a hard-headed and determined, somewhat dogmatic, individual with thirty-five years of doing it my way. Now God is suggesting that if I want to honor His instructions and love my wife like He loves the Church, one of the things I must do is give up my will.

What does that mean? I began to search my mind for all the clever husband sayings that I had been told and immediately remembered something I heard from a coworker just before I was married to Cindy. He told me, "Give up the base hits for the home runs." I immediately knew what this meant and thought that it made sense. Basically, he was explaining that I should give up the things that I don't really care about so that I can get the things that I really do care about. I liked this so much that for many years I used it is as my word of wisdom for soon-to-be-husbands. It seemed like a pretty sound principle. Yet as I revisited this precept, I thought back to the Garden. Would you consider what Jesus gave up for us to be a base hit or a home run? I began to analyze just what Jesus giving up His will for me got him.

First and foremost, it got Him death. That said to me that giving up your life would probably be a home run in that analogy. The beauty of this is that it gave Him a way to be in a closer relationship with His Bride, the Church. He gave up His life so that He could have the kind of relationship He wanted with His bride. Then it hit me like a ton of bricks; I must give up my will if I want the close relationship that I desire with my bride. So I began my mission. I would test this new idea out on many of my friends who are husbands and see how they would respond. What stories would I get? What insight could I glean? After several lunches and afternoon coffees, I was always met with a dead stare, a nod, and a quick transition to a discussion about weekend plans or the weather. It turns out that giving up your will is not a popular idea. I even had one friend who asked,

"Who could do that?" Of course, immediately, I heard the Holy Spirit whisper, "I did."

So, now the difficult road to putting this new revelation into practice begins. It's easier said than done. I can assure you that as soon as you start to give up your will, you will quickly realize how selfish you have been. You also will become keenly aware of how difficult it is to do this. In my case, I was starting the uphill battle of recovering from an affair and the pain I had caused my wife. Of course, I wanted to pay my penance for all I had done, so initially, it was relatively easy to do the little extra things that I didn't do before. I was on-board, whether it was helping with laundry, dishes, house cleaning, grocery shopping, not watching that sporting event on television, not going to a concert, or not overcommitting and continuously being away from my house. I began to understand that giving up my will was more than just what I would add to my plate. It was just as much about what I would take off my plate. This was a difficult concept for me to grasp. At that stage of my life, I was validated by what I did.

I can assure you that your current will is in some way causing separation in your marriage. If you notice in the story of the Garden, Jesus did more than give up His will; He took on the will of the Father. As you begin to give up your will and take on the Father's will for your life and marriage, you will start to understand what loving your wife like He loves the Church looks like. Just as Jesus gave up His will to be in a closer relationship with you, so will your relationship with your wife become more intimate as you give up yours. I speak from experience. I want to make it clear—I do not have this down perfectly. I often fight to do what I want, or even worse, I fight against what I don't want to do. I often think, this must be what Paul felt when he said, in Romans 7:15, "For I do not understand my own actions. For I do not do what I want, but I do the very thing I hate."

My wife would be the first to tell you that I am not perfect at practicing this principle, but I'm positive that she would equally acknowledge that I sure am trying! Even as I wrote this chapter, we discussed how she wanted to go back home to visit her parents for Easter while I wanted to stay home and be at our Church for Easter Sunday. I made it clear that we would stay home and visit her parents some other time, but then I had a trip to the Garden and came out with a different perspective. I have found that when my wife and I have a battle of wills, it always helps to follow Jesus' example and take a trip to the Garden. I love that Jesus not only went to the Garden to pray, but he went in "a little farther" (Matthew 26:39). Sometimes we need to go a little farther to see past our will and find the true heart of the Bridegroom. I'm happy to report that after a bit of time of going farther in the Garden, I was able to happily share with my wife that I would be glad to go to her parents for Easter Sunday. It felt great to give up my will and let her know that I have come in agreement with her desires. In this action, I took on the considerate heart and the will of the Father.

Another area of giving up your will, and I do understand that it may be controversial to say this, may be your over-involvement with ministry. As a servant of the King, of course, we want to say yes to every area we can when it comes to serving Him. He does love a servant's heart, and he loves using you to do his work. But when the ministry becomes more important than your marriage, this will harm your relationship. This mistake in priorities is in opposition to the concept that Jesus gave up His will to be in a closer relationship with us. As I mentioned in earlier writings, I was very involved in ministry and still found myself on the brink of losing my marriage and family. I think it's crucial for us to prayerfully consider any time we're asked to stack on another group activity or area of ministry. Of course, we want to be in agreement with the Father's will, but there also has to be agreement in our home. And truly following the Father's will should result in agreement in the home. If your time of ministry has a place of priority over your marriage, you may be misplacing your talents. Consider the Parable of the Talents. You can read the entire parable in Matthew 25:14–30. I'm specifically drawn to the part about the servant who buried his talents.

> But he who had received the one talent went and dug in the ground and hid his master's money . . . He also who had received the one talent came forward, saying, "Master, I knew you to be a hard man, reaping where you did not sow, and gathering where you scattered no seed, so I was afraid, and I went and hid your talent in the ground. Here, you have what is yours." But his master answered him, "You wicked and slothful servant! You knew that I reap where I have not sown and gather where I scattered no seed? Then you ought to have invested my money with the bankers, and at my coming I should have received what was my own with interest. So take the talent from him and give it to him who has the ten talents. For to everyone who has will more be given, and he will have an abundance. But from the one who has not, even what he has will be taken away. And cast the worthless servant into the outer darkness. In that place there will be weeping and gnashing of teeth" (Matthew 25:18, 20–30).

I don't want to just beat up on the minister types. Over-commitment to any work, play, or selfish indulgences will separate you from the relationship you desire and need with your bride. We can always come up with a reason why we need to work a little longer or have another meeting, but when does it end? When do we realize that our will gets in the way of God's will for our relationship with our wives? When it comes to overcommitment to ministry or work, could it be that if we are committing our talents to areas where the Father hasn't called us or where our wives aren't in agreement, we are in essence burying our talent? If we say yes to the wrong thing, we may be saying no to the right thing. Can we fulfill the call the Lord has for us if we aren't in agreement with our spouses? I love the power of agreement. In Matthew 18:19 it says, "Again I say to you, if two of you agree on earth about anything they ask, it will be done for them by my Father in heaven."

Let's be honest with each other, or at least be honest with yourself right now. How many things are you doing in the name of ministry that are bringing division into your home? How many times have you left the family for a church obligation, and it lead to an issue at home? Maybe this little side track doesn't apply to you, but perhaps it does once you consider it more closely. I want to encourage you to do all the Father is calling you to do, but I would equally encourage you to go to the Garden in prayer to get clarity on whether this is your will or His will.

Let's get back to the lighthearted celebration of what I've found when it comes to giving up one's will. As I mentioned before, giving up your will as an act of living out Christ's love is not only about what you give up, but it's equally about what you will take on. I can remember feeling good about myself when it came to helping with the laundry. I learned how to separate the colors. I knew what went in hot and what went in cold. If you asked me, you would think that I was a professional launderer. (Is that a thing?) Anyway, I would separate, wash, and even throw it all into the dryer at the perfect temp, and then I would call it good.

It all seemed okay until my wife pointed out one issue with my laundry abilities. I immediately jumped to my offended response, "Excuse me? An issue with my laundry abilities? You should be glad I'm even helping with laundry." Yikes! I sounded like a total jerk. She responded, "You are skipping the hardest part." "What do you mean?" I asked. "I'm separating, washing, and drying. This seems like quite a bit of work," I proudly responded. "Yeah, but you're not folding. You're leaving the clothes in the dryer to wrinkle, and you're not folding and delivering the laundry to the appropriate room," she replied. Of course, my response was something like, "Well if you can't appreciate the help, I just won't do it anymore." This all felt like a justified response to what seemed like a lack of appreciation for my colossal sacrifice for the family (sarcasm intended, if you didn't catch it). But then I had a trip to the Garden.

Though I was helping, I wasn't making the impact that I thought I was. I felt like I was doing enough, but it never crossed my mind that I was doing the easiest part. My will wasn't to fold the laundry and deliver the folded laundry to the appropriate rooms. My will was to do what I wanted to do and leave the rest for someone else. Leaving the job unfinished seemed perfectly acceptable until I took a moment to consider why what I was doing wasn't enough. After some time going a little farther into the Garden, I realized that this was an opportunity to give up my will. What was the result of my giving up my will in this matter? First, I spent more time with my wife as she taught me how she wanted stuff folded, which was but another opportunity to give up my will. Once I was thoroughly trained in the way of laundering, I went to work. Today I pull the laundry together from each room, separate laundry, wash laundry, dry laundry, and yes, fold laundry. I have even gotten good at knowing to which room it all goes. I am aware that this is just a small thing. I'm sharing this to help demonstrate that giving up our will isn't always immediate death to our dreams. Sometimes it's the little things that make a big difference.

That being said, here's an example of something that might be a little bigger when it comes to giving up one's will. Probably a year after the affair, I found myself leading worship for a small church in our hometown. My very best friend and beautiful friend of Jesus, Ike Jones, was the interim pastor of this congregation and had asked me to come lead worship. Ike had known my passion for worship since he was in worship bands and settings with me for years. We'll get back to that shortly.

My family had been attending a church that was contributing to our healing, and only being a year out from the day Cindy decided to stay with me, we needed to be somewhere stable when it came to healing the wounds that were in both of us. God had done something miraculous in only a year, but in retrospect, I can tell you that the work wasn't complete. It makes me think of the story in Mark chapter 8. It's the story of the miracle Jesus had done in Bethsaida. "And he took the blind man by the hand and led him out of the village, and when he had spit on his eyes and laid his hands on him, he asked him, 'Do you see anything?' And he looked up and said, "I see people, but they look like trees, walking."Then Jesus laid his hands on his eyes again; and he opened his eyes, his sight was restored, and he saw everything clearly" (Mark 8:23–25). I guess you could say that up to this point I still wasn't seeing very clearly.

So I pulled my family from the church where the healing was happening and decided that I would lead worship at a different church. I need to make it clear that this was my will. This was not my wife's will. As I think back to this time, I remember that she was working really hard to be supportive through her pain. She didn't think it was a good idea for us to change churches. She didn't think it was good for us or our kids, but in the name of "ministry," I did it, and she followed. I did this for a few months, and honestly, the Lord moved in this moment. I saw lives changed and hearts healed, but I wasn't seeing clearly. Our miracle wasn't complete yet. Needless to say, things became rough at home because I was focused on my will, but then I took a trip to the Garden. It's funny how a trip to the Garden always results in a place where you've given up your will, or maybe I should say, a place where you're willing to give up your will. Consequently, I resigned as the worship leader, and we returned to the church we had been attending. More than a decade has passed since we went back, and we still attend Hope Church.

Hope Church has been just that for our family, a place of hope. I am happy to say that the miracle that started eleven years ago is now complete. I can see my wife clearly. I can see who she is, and we can love each other even through disagreement. It's still a journey, and it isn't always easy, but we are together forever. I owe all the praise and honor to Jesus, who started the miracle years ago.

I remember in our premarital counseling, my pastor at the time and his wonderful wife, Steve and Shawn Davis, said something that has stuck with me. He said, "Often, your wife's voice is the voice of the Holy Spirit." I kind of shrugged that off. Of course, at times my wife may say things that do not sound a lot like Jesus (Don't we all?). But the idea that the voice of opposition or agreement coming from your wife may be the Holy Spirit is intriguing to me. Cindy and I have been married for almost 20 years, and that statement from Pastor Steve has proven right more often than not. Remember, it's not just about giving up your will, but it's about taking on the will of the Father in the place of yours for the sake of your relationship. Jesus gave up His will and accepted the Father's will so He could be in a closer relationship with us. Society teaches us that if we strive for what we want, we can attain it, whatever the cost. But Jesus taught that "whoever loses his life for my sake will find it" (Matthew 16:25).

As I mentioned before, I've heard many say that giving up your will isn't fair or even possible. Let me give you a little bit of hope. I'm not perfect at this, but I have been practicing. I can tell you that as you become more comfortable going to the Garden and leaving without your will as the primary motivation in your life, you will begin to see how this positively affects your relationship not only with your wife but, most importantly, with God. I have noticed that over the years, as I have given up my will in even the smallest areas, it has caused my wife to draw nearer to me. It has set an example in my home that now my wife and children are learning to live by. These days, Cindy and I are more inclined to agree than disagree. I find that our desires are more similar as we each spend time in the Garden. It has caused us to have a deeper and closer relationship, which mirrors the way Jesus loves the Church. Consider how giving up your will is one more way you can love your wife like Christ loves the Church.

Ask Yourself

1. When faced with a decision that might involve giving up my will, am I willing to go to the Garden? (I would encourage you to go to the Garden often. The point is to pray for right-mindedness when it comes to a situation and how your will is getting in the way of your relationship. Follow Jesus' model, and go a little farther even when you think you're done. While those around you may be sleeping and unaware, I encourage you to stay awake, focus on prayer, and be ready to give up your will for the sake of relationship.)

2. Am I willing never to assume the miracle is done? (God is always working. Yet if you become complacent, you will find yourself falling back into old, bad habits.)

3. Am I willing to always invite God, through the Holy Spirit, to be part of the process? (You can't do this on your own, and neither can she.)

Let's Pray

Heavenly Father, thank You for Your revelation of the Garden. Thank You for the example You set when it comes to giving up one's will. I want to be like You. I want to put my bride first. I want to put her wants and needs over mine. I want to give up my will because I want to be like You. I want to love my wife the way You love Your Bride. Let Your will, and not mine, be done. I need Your help to love my wife unconditionally, and as I do this, I pray that she begins to love and respect me the way I believe I need. Help me to love my wife like You love the church. I love You. In Jesus' name, amen.

THOUGHTS & REFLECTIONS

CHAPTER THREE

UNCONDITIONAL RESPECT

IS THAT A THING?

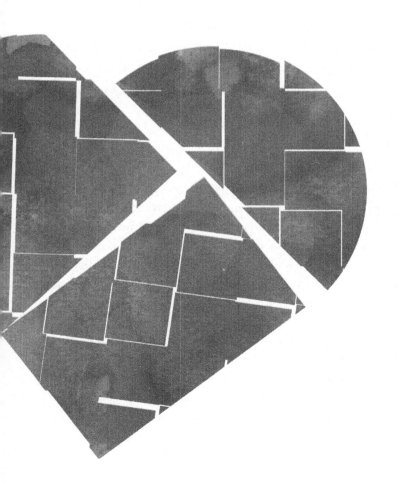

Wives, submit to your own husbands, as to the Lord. For the husband is the head of the wife even as Christ is the head of the church, his body, and is himself its Savior. Now as the church submits to Christ, so also wives should submit in everything to their husbands.

Husbands, love your wives, as Christ loved the church and gave himself up for her, that he might sanctify her, having cleansed her by the washing of water with the word, so that he might present the church to himself in splendor, without spot or wrinkle or any such thing, that she might be holy and without blemish.

Ephesians 2:22–27

I have always been intrigued by this passage. As early as my childhood, I can remember people referring to wives submitting to their husbands. Sometimes it was in jest, and sometimes it was with a seriousness that made the whole room a little uncomfortable. Not until I was an adult did I really read, for the first time, the second part of the message. And it wasn't until about a year after my fall that I pondered what loving my wife like Christ loves the church even looked like.

It sounds easy at first. Love my wife just like Jesus loves me; I can do that. I mean, come on, we all love our wives! All we need for them to do is to understand us, think the world of us, give us free time, don't nag, let us do whatever we believe God is leading us to do, and if they disagree, remember that we are the head of our house, and they need to submit to us. (If you didn't catch it, that was sarcasm again.) The problem with this simplistic view of love is that once you start considering what Jesus' love for the church looks like, you will have a moment of truth that will either compel you to search deeper into yourself to be more like Him or choose to remain in the darkness.

I've spent a lot of time reading and digging into this particular scripture to understand precisely what the Lord is asking of me and all husbands when it comes to loving our wives like He loves His Bride. After all I had done not being the husband I was called to be, I wanted to make sure I properly understood what it meant to do it right going forward. After all of this, I've concluded that we may have been reading the scripture wrong.

My experience for years has been that the Church, especially the men in the Church, have overly focused on men being the leaders of the home. They explained that we are God's appointed priests unto our spouses and children, and they shalt not question that. In a perfect world, yes, families are to follow husbands and trust us with the guidance of our homes. But it is not a perfect world with perfect husbands. Thinking of my own imperfections, I asked myself, *Would I follow someone who didn't know where they were going? Would I be willing to trust someone who led me astray over and over? Do I like following people who lead by demanding respect rather than earning that respect?* The reason we submit ourselves to Jesus is because He has earned a place of respect from us. He hasn't led us down the wrong path. He is the right path. We would follow Jesus anywhere because we know His steps are the right ones. He will lead us to the right place in life where we need to be. Can this be said of your leadership as a husband?

I find myself wondering if maybe we have misunderstood the Ephesians scripture when it comes to submission and love.

Is it possible that we have missed the full meaning? Perhaps we, as husbands, should understand it as instructing us to love our wives like Christ loves the Church, and *then* they will submit to, or should I say respect and follow, us. I think you will understand where I'm coming from if we look at the love of Jesus. Christ's love is unconditional; it doesn't hinge on whether we respect Him. It doesn't even hinge on whether we believe in Him. His love for us was so great that He gave up His life for us *before* we had even sinned. Our submission to Jesus happened as a result of His love for us. I would suggest that it should happen similarly in our marriages. Our husbandly love must come first.

I'm sure you would agree that the love we have for our wives should be unconditional, but there is an old saying about respect and that it is earned. Maybe, if we follow Jesus' model, we should express our love first and in faith that our wives will respond. Though we have all heard of unconditional love, I've never heard of unconditional respect. Our love may be that condition.

I have worked many different jobs in my life, and I have never thought much of supervisors who demanded my respect. Supervisors who expected me to agree with them just because of their position never ranked very highly on my list of favorite bosses. Once I had the opportunity to be the boss, I wanted to make sure that I never had the "because I said so" attitude. I always wanted my employees to understand that I wouldn't ask them to do anything that I wasn't willing to do. I wanted them to know that I had a clear vision of where the company was going, and I had an even clearer view of their role in the company. My employees trusted me with their future in the company because I had proven to them that I knew what I was doing and knew where we were going. I had spent the time reading the handbook. I spent the time consulting my superiors.

I had a complete understanding of the vision for our company. I not only proved to be an effective manager, but I worked to be an effective leader. There is a difference between those two, and figuring out what that means in your house might be the first step to saving your marriage. I once heard Peter Drucker, a fore-father of modern-day people management, say, "Management is doing things right; leadership is doing the right things."[1]

As husbands, we may feel that we are doing things right. But if we want to be the true leaders we are called to be, we may need to stop and ask ourselves if we are even doing the right things. So often, we expect our wives to quickly support us and give us the okay to do whatever we think we need to do. In our minds, we believe that If we say, "God is telling us," then that should be good enough. If they question us at all, then they are disrespecting the call that God has given us. The problem with this philosophy is that our wives, as well as God, know precisely how much time we are reading the Handbook (the Bible) on spiritual leadership. They know how often we are checking with our Supervisor (God) on the direction that our families should go. Why do we expect the person who knows us best to blindly follow us when they know that we've spent next to no time pre-paring for the journey? Would we be willing to follow someone who had not prepared for the journey?

Maybe it's just me, but it seems that often, we as men, would prefer making the wrong decision than asking for help. I know that this was the case for me earlier in my life. But when I look at the life and ministry of Jesus, I see preparation that gave Him direction. When we look at His early ministry, we are challenged to ask our-selves how many times we fasted for forty days before we started a ministry. Jesus was God in the flesh, but His public ministry began

1 Drucker, Peter, *The Essential Drucker,* (New York, NY: HarperCollins, 2001) 228.

after thirty years of preparation. That may say something to us about our need for preparation through the journey of life.

Everyone claims to want to be on the right path, but will they do what it takes to be on that path? We even do mental gymnastics to make it appear we're on that path. It's so easy for us to create a scenario where everything we've always wanted seems to magically line up with what we say is God's will. The hardest part for us is to realize that just because what we are doing isn't bad (maybe it's even work in the church) it doesn't mean it's God's work in our lives. I believe that it's easy for men to generate an idea about something they need to do, and then call it the will of God because it feels necessary. This is very easy to do if you've been in the church very long. You feel like you have a natural ability to recognize if God has something for our lives. As soon we conjure up a seemingly reasonable idea, we decide it's time for us to move our families or leave our families at home while we go on our new mission field. All the while, our wives and our children are at home wondering when they are going to see daddy. When are they going to have their family's spiritual priest minister to them? It is hard to respect and follow the lead of someone who is absent.

You see, gaining the respect that we as men so desperately need and desire takes more than just an expectation. It takes true consideration on our part, extended to our family. That consideration is birthed out of love learned from time spent in preparation to lead. It is birthed by the kind of preparation that was modeled by Jesus. It is found in prayer, fasting, and listening to God. If we want our wives to respect and follow our leadership, then we must first earn that respect with the kind of love that Jesus has extended to us.

ASK YOURSELF

1. What kind of leader am I in my home? Take a moment and describe your leadership compared to how you prefer to be led.

2. Am I setting a godly example to be followed, or am I just expecting my family to follow any and every idea I come up with automatically?

3. What would your life look like if before you jumped in a new direction, you spent time and sought God for His will? How might things change if you sat down with your wife and had a discussion before making decisions?

LET'S PRAY

Heavenly Father, thank You for never-ending revelation and everything that You are teaching me. Thank You for setting an excellent example for me when it comes to getting my priorities straight. Help me not to be driven by what I think my wife and family needs but to be compelled to love unconditionally. Help me to earn the respect that I desire from my wife through love. When it comes to our life and decisions, please give me wisdom to seek Your will and hear from my wife on family matters. I understand that the more I act like You, the more I will love like You, and the more my wife will be drawn to me. Help me to become more like You in all of my interactions, especially those with my wife. Help me to love and treat her the way I want to love and be treated. And ultimately, help me to love my wife like You love the Church. In Jesus' name, amen.

THOUGHTS & REFLECTIONS

CHAPTER FOUR

GOLDEN RING GOLDEN RULE

WHAT DOES YOUR WEDDING RING SAY ABOUT YOUR MARRIAGE?

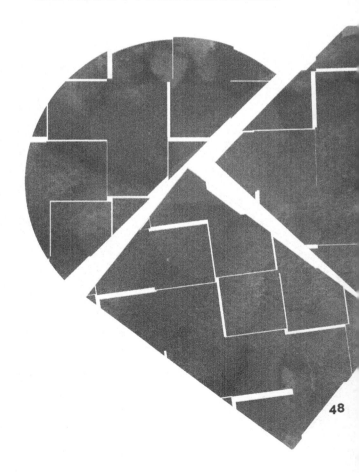

48

"So whatever you wish that others would do to you, do also to them, for this is the Law and the Prophets."

Matthew 7:12

Maybe you've heard of the Golden Rule, and perhaps you haven't. The idea is that we should treat others the way we would like to be treated. This idea comes from the Bible verse quoted at the beginning of this chapter. Whether you are familiar with this scripture or not, it is relatively self-explanatory. It makes a lot of sense if you want to be someone who treats people fairly, is considerate, and is loving.

As I consider how the Golden Rule is applied in my house, it reminds me of an old country song that a friend recently introduced me to. It was a duet by Tammy Wynette and George Jones. The song is called "Golden Ring." The lyrics are simple, and they talk about a golden ring that a young couple came across in a pawn shop. The point was that the ring might have been simple, but what mattered was that the love gave the ring meaning. The golden ring meets the golden rule of love.

If you are married, you probably have some sort of ring. It may or may not be golden these days. Maybe it's rubber, tungsten, titanium, or even a tattoo. But you more than likely have a ring that represents your relationship with your spouses. My ring is rubber because I'm a drummer and my wife likes that the rubber band doesn't make the noise that my previous ring made when I tapped it on the table. I prefer the tones of a tungsten ring against a table, but the rubber ring is just me giving up my will. All jokes aside, in most cases, we put the ring on when we said, "I do," but haven't fully taken into consideration what that ring means. Even as I look down at my ring right now, I find myself thinking about the path that my wife and I have traveled—the life, the love, the pain, and the healing. This is what my ring means to me. It means we are together even after all that we have been through. We have stuck together through everything because we began to apply the principle of the golden rule in our marriage. A successful marriage is when the golden ring meets the golden rule.

I think of all of the times I have counseled and coached my kids, and even employees, on the importance of treating others the way we would like to be treated. Whether I was talking about sibling disagreements or an unruly customer, I have found it very important to consider the person before we respond. Ask yourself what they might be going through that would make them behave the way they are. What kind of consideration would we like to be shown if we were in that person's shoes?

This principle is easy to preach, but it is significantly more challenging to practice. I can think of many times that I haven't treated people the way I want to be treated, even though I have always considered myself a champion of the concept. I'm sure that you would agree that this principle is even more important for Christians. We should be prepared to extend this courtesy to Christians and non-Christians alike since Jesus extended far more to us. It seems so simple in theory, but a challenge in practice. If everyone practiced this principle, it could—no, it would—change the entire world.

Naturally, as I considered the ways that I can love my wife better, I became convicted over my exercise of this principle that I have worked so hard to teach my children. Numerous times I've told them to treat people the way they want to be treated and to love their neighbor as they love themselves, but at the same time, they have watched me not respond similarly to their mom, my wife. I had to ask myself, if I believe we are supposed to treat others the way we want to be treated, then why am I not even trying to practice that principle in my home? If it is possible that treating everyone as we want to be treated would change the world, then unquestionably, I must believe that treating my spouse with this kind of love would change our home. Right?

When I think about how I should apply the Golden Rule, it makes me think about an account from the Bible that details some things Jesus said just before He ascended to Heaven. He was giving His followers instructions about how to proceed after he was gone and how His Spirit, the Holy Spirit, would come to empower them to be witnesses. The verses say, "But you will receive power when the Holy Spirit has come upon you, and you will be my witnesses in Jerusalem and in all Judea and Samaria, and to the end of the earth" (Acts 1:8).

Jesus' followers were already in Jerusalem. He told them that first, they were to be His witnesses in Jerusalem—right where they were. Then He said to move to Judea and Samaria, which were areas farther removed from their home area. Then He finally instructed them to move to the ends of the earth. Jesus started them at home. He didn't say to be His witnesses beginning with the end of the earth. He started with home base, Jerusalem. Earlier in that chapter, Jesus even encouraged

His followers "not to depart from Jerusalem, but to wait for the promise of the Father" (Acts 1:4). So let's take this scripture and translate it into the Paul Harris version: Husbands stay in your home and be with your family until the Holy Spirit comes. After the Holy Spirit comes, be my witness in your home. Tell your wife, your children, and your family about me. Don't just tell them with your words but tell them with your life. Once you have that straight, then go to your work, your church, your city, and be my witnesses. Once you have that down, then be my witnesses to the end of the earth. Don't forget; I want you to stay home until the Holy Spirit comes.

I have always been that guy that when I saw someone on the side of the road, no matter if they needed a tire, sandwich, or a hug, I felt compelled to stop and offer them something. This state of mind was driven by considering how I would feel if I were homeless, helpless, or alone. Don't think I'm perfect. I haven't always stopped. And I haven't been compelled to help in every situation. But I've always at least felt a strong need to make a difference. I have this need to impact another human's world. I mean, who, if stranded on the side of the road, wouldn't want someone to help? If you were hungry and had no money, wouldn't you be thankful if someone showed up with a sandwich? Why don't I feel as compelled to help when I find my wife stranded or alone traveling through life? Why didn't I see that she was hungry? Even as you read this, ask yourself the question, "How is my wife emotionally right now?" Have you ever asked that question?

I remember shortly after the affair, I had happily accepted the grace that both God and my wife had offered me. I was living in freedom from my past and was only looking to the future. I had hit the road to recovery. The chains of hidden sin no longer bound me. I was forgiven. She, my friends, my family, her family, God, and everyone else had forgiven me. I still remember the day after I told Cindy about my infidelity. I was driving to work and had a scripture come to my mind and heart—"Blessed are the merciful, for they shall receive mercy" (Matthew 5:7). It felt like God was saying to me, "Because you have been merciful, you will receive mercy." At that moment, I realized that even in my disobedience and disregard for the vows that I made to God and my wife, God is always true to His word. I was so thankful that in years past, I had not judged others. I had loved others the way I loved myself. I had treated others the way I wanted to be treated. This was the freedom of the forgiveness I was extended. Then after about two weeks of trying to figure out how we would safeguard our marriage so that we could avoid another season of pain like we had just experienced, I realized that telling Cindy about the affair wasn't the hard part; the hard part was yet to come.

I was so caught up in my received forgiveness that I wasn't considering my total disregard in all of these areas when it came to my wife. Had I loved her the way I wanted to be loved? Had I treated her the way I wanted to be treated? Of course, the answer to both is no; I had not. You would think I would have come to this realization reasonably quickly, but I didn't. I was only concerned with the fact that my wounds were healing and initially didn't put myself in Cindy's shoes.

Before the affair, I spent so much time trying to impact the world that I completely lost track of the world that existed inside the four walls of my home. I forgot to apply the Golden Rule at home base before reaching to the ends of the earth. Even as I sit here considering how I still fail at practicing this, I find myself amazed that I could ever have had a sincere concern for total strangers that didn't translate to the way I treated my wife. So how did that happen? How was it possible? I have come up with a one-word answer to this question: selfishness.

Selfishness is the enemy of the Golden Rule in every setting, especially at home. The essence of the Golden Rule is complete *selflessness*. We are typically willing to swallow our pride in a professional environment. Even if we disagree during a business meeting or in the office, we do it in a way that is respectful and considerate. The odds are slim that when you are having a bad day, you show up to work and mistreat your co-workers, clients, or customers. When dealing with that difficult person with whom we attend church, we still find the grace to exchange pleasantries as we pass through the pew. Yet at home, we seem to toss grace out the window.

When we express this selfishness at home, our spouses bear not only the burden of their own day, but they bear the burden of our day as well. The Golden Rule isn't about dumping your issues onto another; it is about considering another's issues and how we would want to be treated in that situation. This principle should ring the truest at home. I would even go as far as to say that if we grasped this idea in our own homes, it would begin to spread out of our front doors and into our neighborhoods, communities, and on and on. What's crazy is that I was ready to move on down the road of forgiveness and never stopped to see my wife stranded on the side of the road. I was willing to admit that I had been selfish in my act of infidelity but somehow didn't immediately realize how selfish I was being when it came to only considering my healing. Yes, we must accept the grace that God offers. We must look to the future and not the past. But are we considering how we would want to be treated in each scenario? Though God's grace is instant, that doesn't mean our wives' is or even should be.

How would I have felt if the tables had been turned? Let me play it out: My wife tells me that she cheated on me. I ask her to stay and say that we can work it out. She immediately finds forgiveness and expects everything to be perfect from now on. She never considers the pain I might feel on each anniversary of her telling me. She never considers the pain I might feel when I hear the name of the guy. She never considers the agony in my mind when I wonder if she still has feelings for him, would she do it again, or what did she like so much about him? If you gave me this scenario, I might say, "Wow, she is selfish." As I said before, the hard part of forgiveness is the journey it takes to get to the complete healing. I thought I was healed, but until I considered my wife's pain, the healing couldn't complete. Until I treated her the way I wanted to be treated, I couldn't fully understand my forgiveness.

Every year, I spend a weekend away with a bunch of my best friends. Whether we get together during the rest of the year or not, once summer arrives, I know that we will be taking a weekend getaway. It just has always been that way. I mean, even before I was married, I was making this trip with the boys. I never thought it was an option not to make the trip, and even worse, I never considered how taking a weekend away might affect my wife and kids. I just scheduled it and did it. Though my wife is gracious enough to encourage me to spend this time with friends, I have never offered that we save some money back so she can go on an annual trip with the girls. She has never even suggested this. She packs my bag, hugs me, and then gets back to the kids. How many hunting trips do we take? How often do we lay on the couch all day watching our favorite sports? (I do this a lot during football season.) How often are our wives left at home to manage while we are out enjoying guy time? How would we feel if the table was turned? What if our wives told us that they would be gone for a weekend getaway once a year? She also will be spending every Sunday afternoon watching her favorite T.V. show. She also will be away for several professional meetings, but when she gets home, she will then need to make time for all of the social clubs she is part of. Oh, and by the way, you need to stay home with the kids so she can do all of these things. Really? Tell me now, do we love our wives like we love ourselves?

I can't answer whether you practice the Golden Rule at home, but I can make some suggestions on how to know if you are. These are the areas where I pray that I can continue to be better. If you don't think your wife is treating you the way you want to be treated, then you should flip the expectation onto yourself. For example, maybe you don't think your wife is respectful to you. Well, perhaps you need to be more respectful to her. Maybe you'd like for your wife to have the dishes done, so the kitchen's not a mess. Well, perhaps you should wash the dishes. Maybe you wish your wife would spend more time doing things you enjoy. Well, perhaps you should spend more time doing the things she enjoys. Maybe you wish your wife would give you a break to have some personal time. Well? (I think at this point you can fill in the rest.)

The beauty of this rule is that as soon as you become selfish, you are no longer practicing the rule. As soon as you start saying, "I have been treating her the way I want to be treated, and she isn't doing anything for me," you have failed to capture the true essence of the rule. The instruction isn't to treat others the way you want to be treated as long as they reciprocate. It plainly states to treat others how you want to be treated.

You may be thinking, why are you picking on guys? Well, for one, I'm a guy. And secondly, I'm a husband. Whether we like it or not, you and I are the ones who were instructed to "love your wives, as Christ loved the church" (Ephesians 5:25). Because of this, we have a responsibility to set the tone for our homes. Jesus gave up His will and His life. I believe that when it comes to being a husband, we should approach our wives the same way. It's not about what we're getting; it's about what we're giving. If our goal as a Christian is to be like Jesus, and it should be, then taking the initiative to live by the Golden Rule is on husbands. Yes, our wives should do the same, but I believe that if we husbands begin to practice the teachings and life of Jesus in our homes, then that love will permeate everything. For the sake of our marriages, we must start practicing the Golden Rule from the inside out. It has to begin in our homes.

Take a second and look down at the ring finger on your left hand (or wherever yours is, if you have one). Take a look at your wedding ring. What does it represent to you? I would suggest that from this day forward, when you see your wedding ring, that you see the Golden Rule. Let your vows represent a selfless approach to being a husband. It is the way Jesus loves you.

1. When it comes to watching T.V. or a movie night, do I suggest something my wife would like to watch, or do I opt-out if it's not something I want to see?

2. When it comes to date night, do I suggest outings my wife enjoys, or does it have to be something that keeps me entertained?

3. When I'm done mowing the lawn, cleaning the garage, and changing the oil (or whatever your chores are), do I then offer to play with the kids, cook dinner, and wash the dishes (or whatever tasks your wife usually handles)?

4. Have I made it a routine of offering pampering to my wife, like massages, with no expectation of sex?

5. Have I encouraged my wife to go shopping or head to the spa while I stay home with the kids with no expectation of her doing the same for my guys and me?

6. Have I made it a point to set back money or make plans so my wife can go on the kinds of trips or nights with friends like I enjoy?

7. Am I a witness for Jesus in my home first and then to the rest of my world?

Heavenly Father, thank You for my wife. Thank You for who she is and all she does. Help me not take her for granted. Help me to realize areas that I am not treating her the way I would want to be treated. Please remind me to put her interests in a place of prominence over mine. Show me ways that I can encourage her and help her so that she knows that I love her. I am so thankful for every opportunity You give me to love my wife the way You love me. Help me to be the bride You desire me to be as You teach me to be the type of husband You require for my wife. Help me to love my wife like You love the Church. In Jesus' name, amen.

THOUGHTS & REFLECTIONS

CHAPTER FIVE

BEHIND THE VEIL

**LOOKING AT MARRIAGE
THROUGH THE EYES OF A BRIDE.**

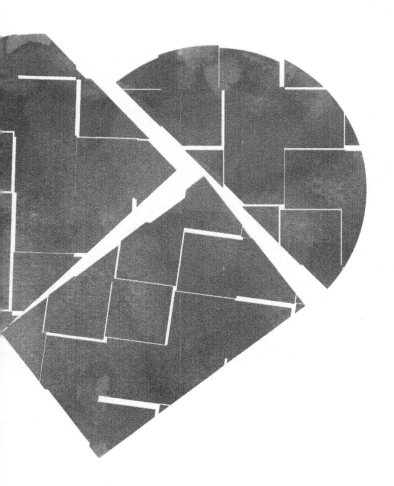

"Let us rejoice and exult
and give him the glory,
for the marriage of the Lamb has come,
and his Bride has made herself ready;
it was granted her to clothe herself
with fine linen, bright and pure"—

for the fine linen is the righteous deeds of the saints.

And the angel said to me, "Write this: Blessed are those
who are invited to the marriage supper of the Lamb."
And he said to me, "These are the true words of God."

Revelation 19:7–9

I recently had a dream. Try to create a mental picture and go there with me for a minute.

I was in a giant church that was full of my family and friends. We all were dressed up and apparently were attendees at a wedding. There must have been thousands of people there; it was packed. I could see the excitement in everyone's faces. Everyone was so happy for the bride. They were all very excited about this wedding ceremony. I wasn't sure who was getting married, so I walked up to someone and asked them, "Who's getting married?" The friend responded with exuberance, "Cindy is!" I thought, "Wait, Cindy is already married; she's married to me." I was bewildered for a minute. Why would my wife be getting married to someone else, and why in the world would all of our friends and family be celebrating it?

Immediately, I was standing alone in a giant, open parking lot. The only thing on the parking lot was a black rectangle, which appeared to be spray-painted. In this box was me. It was me, stripped down in what appeared to be a cloth diaper. I was in this box, moaning and crying for my wife. She was my bride, we were married, but for some reason, she was getting married to someone else. No one seemed to mind or was trying to stop her. Even worse, they were celebrating this marriage. As I watch myself in the box, I thought of biblical stories where people would sit in sackcloth and ashes when they mourned. This was a sackcloth and ashes moment. Then I found myself once again in the church. I was among all of my family and friends who were celebrating the marriage of my bride.

Then I woke up.

Have you ever experienced a dream that is so real or so emotionally moving that you wake up with the feelings you had during the dream? That is how this was. I woke up and immediately began to pray. I asked God, "What is Cindy up to? What is she hiding from me? Who is she going to marry? I was so upset and thought for sure that God was trying to show me something about my wife that I needed to know. He didn't wait to answer. He immediately responded ever so lovingly, "Oh no, you've misunderstood. You were the bride in that dream. I was the Husband. My bride is marrying herself to many other things while she is married to Me. That was Me mourning alone in the box. I mourn the loss of My time with her. I mourn the loss of our intimacy. I mourn the fact that while we are married, she is marrying herself to other things. I'm her first love, and she has left Me. All the while, there is no one trying to stop her. All of her family and friends are celebrating the marriage of her to others while she is still My bride."

That left me emotionally wrecked. While I was concerned that my wife was up to something—she had someone else or she was going to leave me for someone else and all my friends were going to be cool with it—God said to me that I was the wife in that story. That was humbling. My suspicion and feelings of anger immediately melted to a brokenness and sadness. I immediately began searching my heart. What am I marrying myself to? What am I giving my time to? What am I giving my intimacy to? What am I giving my heart to? The answer to all of these questions is this: plenty. I have married myself to plenty of things that have pushed my Bridegroom into the box that I painted for Him in an empty and desolate parking lot off-site. While I'm celebrated for these marriages, He sits in sackcloth and ashes and mourns over His bride. What kind of bride am I? What would I do if my wife treated me as I am treating my Husband? I think we all know how we would respond, but He sits and mourns and waits for us to return to our first love.

Over my life, I have grown to understand God in his role as Father. I have never had issues with viewing Jesus as my friend; we are in a relationship. That being said, I have found it interesting that more often than not, God talks to me as my Husband. I know this might be awkward for some of you, but each of us, regardless of gender, is part of the Bride of Christ. He is looking for a Bride who is wearing that beautifully spotless gown. The gown that His sacrifice made spotless. Though I have always been a pretty sensitive guy and had no issue getting in touch with my feminine side, I still found it odd to think of God the Husband. God the Father, yes. God the Savior, yes. God the Husband, that was a challenge for me. Anyway, on my journey to become a better husband, he has come to me as a Husband to help me understand what it looks like to be a great wife.

I'm sure that when you read the title of this chapter, you initially thought, *of course, Paul. That's the point—put my bride first.*

Well, yes, but the title of this chapter goes much deeper than that. I understand that we, as husbands, all have different needs and different love languages, if you will. At the end of the day, we all want to feel valued and necessary. That is a basic human need. If we don't feel valued, we have a hard time finding purpose in our lives. I would be the first to admit that I have always put a lot of pressure on my wife to make me feel necessary. I often would lose motivation to succeed when I felt my wife didn't love me the way I needed to be loved. I would become depressed if I felt as though she wasn't giving me the respect I thought I deserved. I needed her to be more affectionate. I needed her to be more intimate. I needed her to speak my love language. I struggled with this. I couldn't gain traction in my life because I would become distraught over the fact that I didn't think my wife loved me the way I needed to be loved. I put her in charge of all of my happiness. No human being can handle that kind of pressure. The more I needed, the less she wanted to give. The more I prayed that God would change her heart, the more hardened it seemed to become. This all changed one night while I was begging God to change her so that she would be the wife I always dreamed of.

Make her more intimate, I would request in prayer. Make her more affectionate. Make her more supportive. I confided in God how I was broken-hearted that my bride didn't love me the way I needed to be loved. I continued to go on about how I just needed him to change her heart. Please soften her heart, God, I prayed. My bride doesn't love me the way I want to be loved. My bride doesn't make intimacy with me a priority. My bride doesn't stop to just talk. My bride doesn't put me first. Then in my party of self-pity, God softly and gently responded, "Now you know how I feel." All of a sudden, in a way that only

God can do, He put everything in perspective—His perspective. While I whined about how my wife wasn't treating me the way I needed to be treated, He turned it back on me. I immediately knew that the issue wasn't my wife; the issue was me. If I wanted my wife to love me the way I want to be loved, I not only had to be the model husband, but I needed to model what being a great bride looks like. I had to be a great bride to be a great husband.

All my life, I have heard Christians referred to as the Bride, and I have always believed that marriage between men and women mirrors the relationship between Christ and his Church. But in one second, God had this way of making things very clear without ever making me feel condemned. He just simply said, "Now you know how I feel." I immediately was sympathetic to His pain. I knew what it felt like to be a husband that wants more time from his bride. I understood God's desire for His Bride. I could identify with the fact that He yearned for more of me; His bride.

Now, every time I start feeling sorry for myself when it comes to how I think I should be treated, I immediately ask, "What kind of bride am I being"? What am I marrying myself to? Let's be the bride to our Husband that we want our wives to be. Let us be intimate with Him. Let us be aware of His love language. The Bible says that He is jealous for us. He wants you and only you. I want to encourage you to practice putting God in your place when you start feeling sorry for yourself when it comes to what you think you need and what you think your wife cannot provide. Are you the bride that you want? Are you modeling what being a good wife looks like? I can't be the family or friend that celebrates the marriage of an already-married bride while her bridegroom mourns her loss.

ASK YOURSELF

1. Have I put my wife in charge of my happiness? (We often need specific actions or responses from our spouses to feel the way we think we need to feel. Focus on your relationship with Jesus and allow Him to guide you into true joy and happiness.)

2. Am I focusing on developing an increasingly intimate relationship with God? (Be more intentional when it comes to your relationship with God. Ask yourself what you need from your bride and give that to Jesus. Is it more time, more intimacy, more respect, more love, more conversation? Whatever it is, when you find yourself needing more from your wife, that is the time you should give more to God.)

LET'S PRAY

Heavenly Father, thank You so much for your desire to be in relationship with me. Thank You for my wife. I love who You have made her to be. I love who You have made us to be. I'm sorry for neglecting You. Help me to love You the way I want to be loved. Help me to be the bride to You that I want my wife to be to me. As I seek You first, I ask that You give me the desires of my heart. Help me to love my wife like You love the church. In Jesus' name, amen.

THOUGHTS & REFLECTIONS

CHAPTER SIX

GRACEFULLY HERS

EXCHANGING COURTEOUS GOODWILL FOR HER WEAKNESS.

But he said to me, "My grace is sufficient for you, for my power is made perfect in weakness." Therefore I will boast all the more gladly of my weaknesses, so that the power of Christ may rest upon me.

2 Corinthians 12:9

I have always been a fan of this verse in 2 Corinthians, especially the idea of God's power working best in weakness. His grace is all we need. In this twelfth chapter, the author of 2 Corinthians, the Apostle Paul, was discussing his thorn in the flesh, and he had asked God multiple times to remove this from him. God's response was basically that His grace was enough and that it worked best when Paul was weak.

What is grace? When I look up the definition of grace, I find many, and honestly, they all could apply to marriage. As I dug a little deeper into the definitions, I found one that sounded like the grace that God offers His bride.

"Grace: The free and unmerited favor of God, as manifested in the salvation of sinners and the bestowal of blessings."[2]

Wow! It's free and unmerited favor. Though we don't know what Paul's thorn in the flesh was, I'm convinced that it doesn't really matter. God's response to it was that His grace was all that the Apostle Paul needed. God wasn't worried about the issues Paul was having. He wasn't distracted by his weakness. It sounds like God kind of used Paul's weakness as an opportunity to be the Hero in his story. Could God have

---

[2] Grace, Definition 3, https://www.lexico.com/en/definition/grace (Accessed December 5, 2019).

performed a miracle and removed the thorn that Paul seemed so desperate to separate from himself? Absolutely! But instead, He used it as an opportunity to have Paul depend on Him. I love that Paul responded, "I will boast all the more gladly of my weaknesses" (2 Corinthians 12:9). If God says that His power works best in my weakness, then let me tell you about my weakness so that the power of Christ can work through me.

There is so much that stands out to me when I consider God's response to Paul's prayer. God didn't perform the miracle the way Paul asked for it. God responded with grace to endure the struggle, not a miracle of removal. He didn't judge him and respond with a list of things he could do to overcome the issue. God simply responded with grace and power, perfect power. At that moment, Paul understood that the love and grace that God had for him superseded his need to relieve himself of his struggle. Maybe Paul felt as though this thorn was causing separation in his relationship. Perhaps the enemy had convinced him that as long as he struggled with this thorn, he could never have the relationship he was supposed to have with God. God's response was, nope, my grace is enough. My power works best when you have issues. God's powerful nature is magnified in our weakness. His love is magnified. His mercy is magnified. His peace is magnified. He is more himself in our lives when we allow him to handle our pain, our struggle, and our weakness in His way.

As I consider what this looks like, I can't help but think of God as this superhero who's superpower grows when those who need Him acknowledge their need and allow Him to have it. Our failures and weakness make opportunities for His might to be displayed. He isn't put off by our mistakes.

He isn't frustrated by our failures. He works best under these circumstances. He wants to save the day. He wants us to rely on Him. He wants us to allow His grace to win the day in our lives, allowing our missteps to be an opportunity to prove His unconditional love for his bride.

All of you guys, forty years old and older, will get this next reference. Some of the younger husbands may be familiar too. When I was a kid, there was an old cartoon that I watched called Popeye. Popeye was a sailor, and he had a girlfriend named Olive Oyl, a friend named Wimpy, and an arch-rival named Bluto or Brutus, depending on which era of Popeye you were watching. Popeye was a relatively tough guy, but when he ate spinach (I'm sure this was some conspiracy to try and get kids to eat spinach), he would grow extra big muscles and was utterly undefeatable. I imagine my weakness is something like spinach for God. As God steps in to work through my weakness, like Popeye eating spinach, His full strength is on display. God's strength is made perfect. The more I step out by admitting weakness, the more He has room for His strength to work. I know this may be a little cheesy. But if every time you think of Popeye, you remember that your weakness is God's spinach, then I will claim success.

As I consider yet another way I'm to emulate the love that Jesus has toward my wife, I ask myself, *Is my grace enough? Does my power work best in my wife's weakness?* I would love to tell you that yes, when my wife struggles, I look past it and only love unconditionally. I would like to say that I never get upset with her issues. I would love to tell you that I never get frustrated with her failures, but if I told you that I would be lying. I am sure I have failed and spent time judging her because of what I perceive as her failures, weaknesses, or shortcomings. I have looked down on her because she didn't respond the way I thought she should or didn't act the way I think she should act toward me. I haven't allowed my grace to be enough. I haven't been empowered by her weakness. More often than not, I have made her feel worse about her weaknesses. I have made her feel more insecure about her insecurities. As Paul asked for God to remove his issue, God did anything but make it about Paul's issue. His response was grace. I can confess that my response hasn't always been grace.

So, what I can do to be more like Jesus when it comes to offering grace? I can only think about my beautiful wife. I think about all the times that I thought I was helping by pointing out areas where I thought she could be better. Even this week, I gave her advice about issues, her thorns in the flesh. But that's not how Jesus loves His bride. Instead, I should have focused on grace and being empowered to be more like Jesus by her weakness. What does that look like? I'm working through this even as I type. I think it looks like my not having a comment on her weakness, but only grace. Only offer free and unmerited favor in the face of all issues. It doesn't make sense. It's not fair. It's precisely the way that Jesus loves His bride. When my wife fails, instead of telling her how to respond, I don't even focus on her failure. I immediately offer grace; it's enough. I'm reminded of 1 Corinthians 4:20 that says, "For the kingdom of God does not consist in talk but in power." We often spend time talking about the issue rather than bringing the kingdom of heaven to the matter. God spent almost no time talking about Paul's issue. Instead, He just responded with grace.

Another of the numerous definitions of grace that stood out to me was essentially, courteous goodwill. Have I been responding to my wife's weakness with courteous goodwill?

Courteous goodwill and respectful kindness are the ways God responds to our failures. I'm ashamed to say that I have often responded to her issues with anything but respectful kindness. Yet at this moment, I am compelled to change. I am compelled to be more like Jesus. I desire to respond to my wife's thorns with grace. I long to be empowered through her weakness.

1. Do I naturally respond with grace when my wife acts or responds in a way that I know is wrong? If not, how can I plan to change my behavior?

2. Do I spend more time trying to lecture my wife about her issues than I do finding ways to love her?

3. Does my strength of love, forgiveness, and compassion become perfect through my wife's struggles? If not, what do I imagine that might look like in my life?

4. Will I watch an episode of Popeye, so I know what the heck Paul is talking about?

LET'S PRAY

Heavenly Father, thank You so much for Your grace. Thank You so much for being strong in my weakness. I pray that You are glorified as I allow You to love me through my failures. I ask for the strength to love like You in all ways. I pray that I spend more time bringing Your kingdom of love, peace, and grace to my responses. You are such a great example of how I should respond to my wife and her failures. Let me become more like You. Let me love like You. I pray that my strength as a husband will grow as I offer grace in response to her weakness. I pray that I will spend time pursuing Your heart so I can have her heart. Help me to love my wife like You love the Church. I love You. In Jesus' name, amen.

THOUGHTS & REFLECTIONS

CHAPTER SEVEN

STAY AND PRAY

**THERE ARE TWO WAYS TO ARGUE:
YELL AND LEAVE OR . . .**

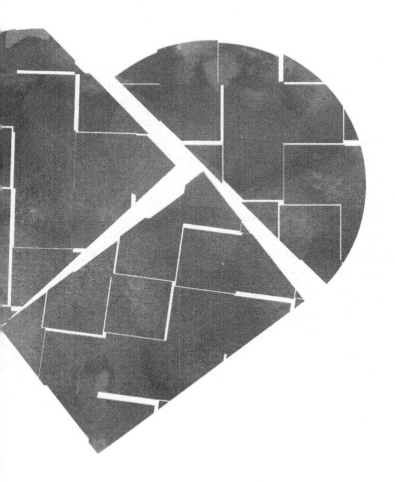

Who is to condemn? Christ Jesus is the one who died—
more than that, who was raised—who is at the right
hand of God, who indeed is interceding for us.

Romans 8:34

I am familiar with the saying, "The family that prays together, stays together." You've probably heard it too. Yet I admit to you that I am hit or miss when it comes to gathering my family and praying. I do pray with them individually more often, but it's not a daily routine.

I feel like the New Living Translation of Romans 8:34 draws a clearer picture. In that translation, it replaces the word "interceding" with the word "pleading." It immediately causes me to have a mental picture of Jesus pleading on my behalf. He sees the struggle I have, and he doesn't want me to fail. He doesn't want me to hurt. He doesn't want me to have the wrong idea of who I am to, and in, Him. He sees my insecurities, and He pleads with the Father on my behalf. I sometimes wonder what He is saying about me. Is he saying, "Please let Paul fully understand the love I have for him"? Is it "Please let Paul come to realize the dreams I have for him"? Or could it be, "Please let Paul not be overcome with temptation"?

I can imagine a hundred things He might be praying for me because of His love. I can envision Jesus pleading for my freedom from the things that so easily get me off track. I love the fact that even after He gave His life, rose from the dead, and ascended to heaven, He doesn't stop with the love. Jesus continues to pray for us. He continues to bring our needs before the Father.

In Matthew 6:8, it says that the "Father knows what you need before you ask him." When I consider the idea of knowing my needs before I ask, it makes me think of a surgeon's assistant. In the middle of a surgery, the surgeon knows what he needs, but he doesn't have time to hunt it down. As he takes care of his patients' body, he will call out "scalpel," and the assistant will hand it to the surgeon. Over time, the surgeon's assistant doesn't need to wait for the surgeon to call out for the next necessary instrument. The surgeon's assistant has the tool already in hand and ready before it's requested. The surgeon's assistant knows the surgeon's need before the surgeon asks. God is far from just some assistant, but as we cry out, He doesn't need to waste any time looking for what we need. He already has it in His hand and is ready to give it to us.

I love that idea when I consider Jesus as our Husband, our Bridegroom. He knows our needs before we ask. He prays for us continuously. He knows what is best for us, and he prays that into us. I love this idea of him pleading for us because it comes with a revelation of His empathy. The facts are that the Father clothed himself as the Son and now knows what we need because he has lived the life we now live. He spent time on earth. He suffered temptation. Hebrews 2:18 states, "For because he himself has suffered when tempted, he is able to help those who are being tempted." He knows our pain, and now He prays for us. And the Father responds by helping us endure through the testing and suffering. He is empathetic with us.

Honestly, as I consider Jesus' love for His Bride, it seems to be founded in empathy. He understands our pain and shares in it by pleading to the Father on our behalf. Praying for your wife like Jesus prays for his bride is a principle that starts with empathy. It's hard to admit, but as we continue in marriage, it is very easy to lose any empathy you may have had for your spouses. As each year passes, we see the same problems. We hear the same complaints. Instead of considering how we might help her with her problem, we just quietly wonder if she'll ever get over it. Will she ever stop complaining about that? Why is she so dramatic? Why doesn't she learn from her mistakes? Even as I wrote this, the Holy Spirit reminded me of Matthew 7:5 that says, "You hypocrite, first take the log out of your own eye, and then you will see clearly to take the speck out of your brother's eye." I am such a hypocrite. I'm so thankful that these examples are not the way that Jesus responds when I complain about the same things, make the same mistakes, or respond dramatically to something that happens that I don't like or expect. That's just not the kind of Husband He is.

Jesus' example of how He loves the Church when it comes to praying for His Bride is an empathetic approach. Let me illustrate how this can apply to my marriage. Instead of getting frustrated with my wife's needs or failures, what might change for the better if I were empathetic and asked myself, "How can I help her with that?" I know that most of the time there is nothing we can do to help our wives, by action or word, when it comes to their struggles. But we can listen, try to understand, and pray. We can plead to the Father on their behalf. Have you ever asked your wife how you can pray for her? Sometimes the tensions of marriage get so tight that a husband might be afraid to ask that question.

Among my many conversations about marriage, I remember what one struggling husband told me. He explained that he began to ask his wife how he could pray for her. At first, he was fearful of how she would respond. He honestly didn't want to ask her because he didn't want to hear her remind him of all the areas he needed to change, that she didn't love him, or that she couldn't forgive him. He was afraid to hear her heart. But as he began to seek the heart of the Father and ask for the kingdom to come to his marriage, he felt as though he needed to ask his wife how he could pray for her. As she began to share her concerns and needs, he felt his heart respond with love instead of fear. I guess this makes sense as in I John 4:18, we are taught that "perfect love casts out fear." In his desire to bring the kingdom of heaven into his marriage, the perfect love of the Bridegroom came to his marriage. He was no longer worried about what his wife might say she needed prayer for. He was no longer resentful or tired of hearing her needs or complaints. Instead, the perfect love of the kingdom of heaven changed his heart.

At times in marriage, we convince ourselves that it is our spouses who needs to change. Yet as we invite heaven into our home, the kingdom arrives, and we realize that we were the problem all along. What might change if we open ourselves up to feel her pain like Jesus feels ours? What if we sincerely prayed for her? This next suggestion might make you uncomfortable, but if this book hasn't made you uncomfortable yet, it is now time. I want to suggest you lay hands on your wife and pray out loud for her. It's one thing to pray for her when you are in your car or silently when you lay down at night. But there is something different about the spoken word. Proverbs 18:21 says, "Death and life are in the power of the tongue," and Mark 16:18 says, "they will lay their hands on the sick, and they will recover." I don't practice this as often as I should, but I am learning that there is something about praying out loud and touching my wife when I pray for her that changes the atmosphere.

There have been times when we were not getting along,

and we were about to disobey the command not to "let the sun go down on your anger" (Ephesians 4:26). I had two options for how I could react in these moments: I could yell and leave, or I could stay and pray. Though I haven't always responded correctly, there are moments, more now than there used to be, where I stopped and prayed out loud for us, and it changed the mood. It brought a calm and peace that none other than the Holy Spirit can bring. This is not easy to do when the disagreement is at a place that seems like there is no happy resolution, but I can assure you that even if it's just in your heart, you will feel a change in the atmosphere. There is a shift that comes when we pray. There is a change that happens when we intercede on behalf of another. I have seen this happen in real-time. I have watched a disagreement with my wife become a place of reconciliation when I decided to stop and pray for her.

I would suggest starting to pray for your wife each night before bed. Hold her and plead with heaven on her behalf. Maybe you don't know what to say, and I get that it can be a little awkward when you are starting this. Before we end this chapter, we will pray together for our wives.

As I consider how praying for my wife during a disagreement can change the atmosphere, I am reminded of the prayer that Jesus taught us in Matthew 6:9–13—The Lord's Prayer. Many of you reading this have recited it in Sunday School or special church services. Have you ever truly considered what is being asked, or has it become something you merely quote? It honestly is the perfect prayer. Just in case The Lord's Prayer isn't something you are familiar with, I will share with you my rendition of it. If even all you can muster is to pray this prayer, it is enough. The following is the Paul Harris version.

Father, who is in heaven,

Holy is your Name.

I ask for Your kingdom to come and Your will be done in our world like it is in heaven.

Please give me the bread I need for today.

Forgive me of my sins as I forgive those who have sinned against me.

Lead away from temptation and deliver me from evil.

Yours is the kingdom, the power, and the glory forever. Amen.

One of my favorite parts of that scripture is where He prayed, "Your kingdom come, your will be done, on earth as it is in heaven" (Matthew 6:10). We could spend a lot of time considering how to do things on earth like they are in heaven, but since we are discussing loving our wives, we probably should stay within the context of marriage. What if we prayed that portion of The Lord's Prayer every day? What would our marriages look like if we asked God to let His kingdom come and for His will to be done in our marriages like things are in heaven? What impact would that have? I'm sure we all have our preconceived ideas of what heaven is like. I can assure you that when I compare my idea of heaven with the reality of my marriage, there are a lot of areas where I need to ask God to send His kingdom. As we pray for our wives, we are inviting the kingdom of heaven into our homes and our relationships. As His kingdom of peace comes, we have a marriage of peace. As His kingdom of love comes, we have a marriage of love. As His kingdom of joy comes, we have a marriage of joy.

One more significant thing to keep in mind when you are praying: there will be times you find yourself praying for your wife to change, or that God will do a work in her; fight that urge. The last thing you want to do is to condemn your wife while praying for her. I think it's important to pray without condemnation. I can remember when I first started changing the way I prayed. I would pray for God to change her heart toward me or ask Him to deliver her from whatever oppression I thought she was experiencing. I found that this just made me frustrated with her, and then I would pray about the things that were frustrating me. This is not the heart of what we are doing here. When Jesus prays for us, he invites the kingdom into our relationship. Rather than praying for changes in the problems, I encourage you to pray for the Holy Spirit to infiltrate your relationship with your wife. This makes me think of another dream that I had:

I was in a church building. I was standing at the back of the building. The stage was in front and to the right of me. I noticed to my left that there was a guy who was wearing a mask that looked like a cartoon character smiling, lingering around the children's area. I had this feeling like he was up to no good. I decided to approach him to ask him what he was doing there, but he wouldn't respond. He just tried to move away from me. At this point, I felt like I needed to escort him out of the church, so I softly put my arms around him in a bear hug and started walking him out of the church. I escorted him out in front of the congregation.

As I walked with him, I was looking for someone I recognized as security to help me. Approaching the exit, I realized that I had quite the entourage growing around me. Once we were in the parking lot, I let go, and he immediately dropped to the ground. I moved around to the front of him to see if there was something I needed to do to help. As I watched him, he shrunk down and became a small child. I would guess he was around two or three years old, and the only thing he wore was a cloth diaper. He no longer had the mask, and his face would go back in forth from ordinary to what I can only describe as demonic.

I heard him try to cast out a demon from himself. He said, "Evil spirit come out of me in Jesus' name," but nothing happened. His face kept distorting. He looked at the crowd and looked at me, so I just repeated it with him. I said, "Evil spirit come out of him in Jesus' name." Again, nothing happened. I immediately felt self-conscious and questioned my walk with the Lord as the demon mocked me for not being able to cast him out. I then began to do the only thing I could think to do, and that was to ask the Holy Spirit to come. As I repeated, "Holy Spirit come, Holy Spirit come," a wind began to blow, and it started pulling the demon out of the guy.

I know that's a long dream just to make a point, but here's the lesson I learned from that dream: often we pray against things so the desired change will come when all we need to do is invite the Holy Spirit to come into a situation. Instead of casting out the demon, invite the Holy Spirit to come. Instead of pointing out what changes your wife needs to make, invite the Holy Spirit to come. Let that be our prayer. Again, I'm not perfect at this and continue to practice. Yet I have seen what it looks like when we pray for the Holy Spirit to come into a relationship, a job, or any part of our lives. It looks like the kingdom of heaven come to earth.

ASK YOURSELF

1. Do I currently have a routine of prayer for my wife? If not, what pattern should I start that reflects Jesus' prayer for me?

2. How might outcomes change if I stop my next spousal argument with prayer instead of being offended or defensive?

3. What can I do today to encourage the kingdom of heaven to be revealed in my relationship with my wife?

LET'S PRAY

(In the prayer below, insert your wife's name where the space is provided. Sincerely pray this for your wife, even daily, if you feel led. I am convinced that as you pray for your wife, you will begin to see the kingdom of heaven fill your home.)

Heavenly Father, thank You so much for designing (_____) just for me. You created her to be strong where I am weak, and weak where I am strong. Thank You for having me in mind when You made (_____). I ask You to bring peace to my wife's mind. Set her free from any insecurities that are keeping her from experiencing the purpose You have for her. Holy Spirit, come to our marriage, come to our relationship, and come to our disagreements. Make all things new like only You can do. Let Your kingdom come and Your will be done in our marriage as it is in heaven. God, please give me Your heart for (_____). Let me see her the way You see her. Let me hear her the way You hear her. Let me love (_____) the way You love her. Instead of focusing on being right, help me to be okay to be wrong. Help me to love (_____) like You love the Church. In Jesus' name, amen.

THOUGHTS & REFLECTIONS

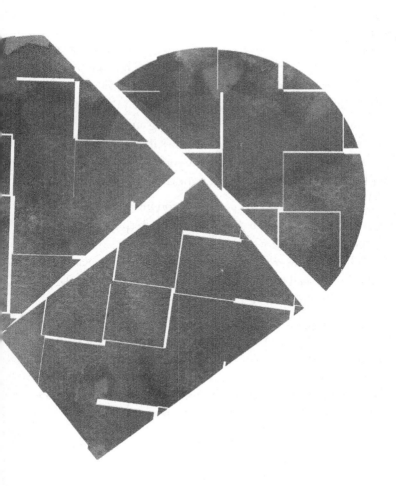

CHAPTER EIGHT

GUILTY UNTIL PROVEN INNOCENT

YEAH, I KNOW IT'S BACKWARDS.

But he was pierced for our transgressions;
he was crushed for our iniquities;
upon him was the chastisement that brought us peace,
and with his wounds we are healed.

Isaiah 53:5

As the Holy Spirit began revealing the heart of Ephesians 5:25 to me and teaching me what it looked like to love my wife like Jesus loves the Church, the majority of it made sense to me. You know, pray for her, love her, and honestly even die for her seemed like apparent options when it came to ways that I should emulate Christ's love. Then there was the day that all changed. I still remember sitting and praying, "God, I need more than just a couple of chapters if you want me to write an entire book on the ways that you love the Church and how I'm supposed to use that as a template for loving my wife."

So, I asked Him for a deeper revelation into the ways He loves and loved the Church. He immediately responded with, "Take the blame." "Take what blame?" I wondered. "All of it," His still small voice answered. I began to ponder exactly what that looked like. It looked like a blameless Man, a blameless God, dying for the sins of a guilty man. It looked like someone who was right, taking the consequence for being wrong, all the while not defending himself. It looked like not arguing to be right even though He was. It looked like Jesus not fighting to get justice for himself but dying so I could be justified. He loved the Church so much that He suffered the consequences of a crime He didn't commit. He loved the Church so much He took the blame.

I began to consider what this might look like to Jesus. How did His humanity feel about taking responsibility for a crime He didn't commit? As I pondered how it might feel to be accused of a crime that I didn't commit, I thought back to a time, as a child, where I was accused of something that I didn't do. I was five years old, and someone hit a girl on the playground. It wasn't me. Somehow in the madness of the screaming of children and the teacher trying to break up the crowd and determine who the guilty party was, the little girl, through her tears, pointed me out as the guilty party. The teacher told me to go stand in the hall, next to my classroom door, with the girl that had accused me. She would settle it all after recess. I tried to defend myself, to no avail. So I walked to the spot in the hall next to my classroom and stood, awaiting the verdict.

I still remember my feelings at that moment. I was scared. I was nervous. What would I say when the teacher came back? Would she believe me? I wanted so badly to defend myself, but I felt that the result was inevitable; I was going to get a paddling. (Yes, those were the days when we still got spankings in school.) I was going to pay for a crime I didn't commit. I distinctly remember that the little girl had a red rash on her face. She had this rash for as long as I remember seeing her at school. As I stood next to her, hoping she would have a better recollection of who hit her, a teacher walked past. She asked me, "Did you do that to her?" She was referring to the fact that she had red marks on her face, and apparently, this teacher had heard through the teacher grapevine that I had hit the girl. Not only was I being accused of hitting a little girl, but now my story was spreading through the teaching staff with worsening charges. I had now not only hit a girl, but I had scarred her face for life.

What made matters worse is that the girl wasn't saying anything to confirm that I hadn't done it; she just stood in silence. Even as I think back on this, I am remembering the fear I had and the desire to defend myself to make right the wrong that was happening. How would this end? Will the teacher believe me? Will the girl speak out and defend me? Would I be punished? What will the teachers think? What will my parents say? Back in that day, if you got a paddling at school, many of us also got a spanking at home. So, in addition to the looming punishment at school, there was a chance I would also get spanked at home for something I hadn't done.

Thankfully, once it was all said and done, I was vindicated and didn't have to suffer the consequences for something I didn't do. We never found out who had hit the little girl. Once the recess teacher came back to deal with us, the little girl decided to speak up and defend me. To you, little girl that I didn't hit in kindergarten, thank you.

Fast-forward twenty years, and I decided to honor a commitment to my relationship with God that I made as a child. It wasn't this crazy, loud moment, but as I worked to make peace with the creator of the universe, the twenty-five-year-old version of me made the decision that I wanted a real relationship with Jesus. I had decided to leave life as I knew it and the people I loved to go live with my grandma. She was a strong, godly woman who was the matriarch of our family when it came to spiritual things. When I moved in with her, I began to do two things pretty much: work and go to church. I spent all of my extra time in prayer and reading the Bible. In this time of my life, I experienced what it really meant to work out your own salvation. I also began to understand better who Jesus was. I wanted more than just an idea of who He was; I wanted to know Him personally. I wanted to be His friend.

Even though I was raised in church and had a working understanding of what the Cross represented in my pursuit of a relationship with Him, I came face to face with Jesus, the One who was punished for a crime He didn't commit. He stood before the Sanhedrin (a court made up of religious leaders in ancient Judaism) as they questioned and accused Him. His story had spread, and the charges began to build against Him. He now stood, awaiting His fate.

I wondered if He was hoping someone would defend Him. I wondered if he, too, was shocked at how these religious leaders were accusing Him of things He hadn't done. I knew that place, emotionally. I looked into the eyes of the Person who stood where I had stood when I was a five-year-old boy. I looked into the eyes of a Person who didn't hit me, but would ultimately be hit for me. All of a sudden, I identified with Him on a different level. I understood what it was like to be accused of something I didn't do. I understood the fear that comes with being misunderstood and mislabeled as the guilty party. I identified with the uncertainty of the punishment that might occur. I then realized that our story, though similar at the beginning, had a much different outcome; no one came to His defense. No one set the story straight. Would I have spoken up like the little girl in my case and told the truth, or would I have maintained my silence and let Him take the beating for a crime He didn't commit? Would I have defended Him or stayed quiet? He never defended himself. He took the blame.

I'm now much older than that twenty-five-year-old who recognized what my Savior did for me when He took the blame. As I sit here contemplating why God wanted this to be one of the chapters in a book on how to love your wife, the fog that was created by a need to be right started to clear out. God wants us, as husbands, to see clearly how our love is to emulate His love. The humanity of Jesus may have wanted justice for himself, but His deity was looking to create a means to obtain justice for humankind. The part of me that is concerned with myself always wants justice for me, but as I consider having a love like Jesus, my self-centered justice transforms into a benevolent justice that considers my marriage over myself. I start seeing a good that is greater than my needs.

I was recently talking with a buddy of mine about our relationships with our wives. In a lot of ways, our conversations have inspired me to continue on the path of writing this book. (As an aside, when you feel God is leading you to do something, you often will be met with opposing voices in your head. I encourage you to ask God to surround you with people who will encourage you to do what He has asked you to do.) My buddy was telling me about the relational growth between him and his wife. God had revealed to him new ways to approach spousal disagreements. He said to me that his current revelation was, "Always assume you're wrong." Of course, as I heard him say that I heard the Holy Spirit whisper through his smile, "It's time for the chapter on taking the blame."

My buddy told an all-too-familiar story of how, when he and his wife disagree, he was focused more on helping her understand where he was right instead of identifying where she was saying he was wrong. I have done this so many times, and it never ends the way I expect it to. I thought back to all the times that I've argued with my wife when she said things about me that I don't think are true. My mind was flooded with times she told me what I was thinking, how I see situations that I don't agree with, and how I've let loose anger-filled yelling in my defense. I began to wonder if God was saying what I thought He was saying. Was he suggesting that in these moments, I should assume a position of being wrong when I know I'm right? Is He suggesting that I take the blame for something I didn't do? Is He suggesting that by doing so, I am loving my wife like He loves the Church? I think the answer to these questions is a resounding yes!

Maybe today, you feel like you're in a place of misunderstanding with your wife. You don't think she gets you. You're standing in your life's hall, waiting on the verdict, and you have convinced yourself that she is your accuser. Or maybe in your mind, she is the teacher who will determine whether you are guilty or innocent when it comes to actual actions or assumed intentions. My word for you is that there is hope when you begin to practice this principle on your journey to love your wife like Christ loves the Church. You may be just like the five-year-old me. I knew I was right, but nothing I could say would change the mind of the teacher. Then there is the twenty-five-year-old me who met a Man who came to my defense and took the blame for me. He brought justice to a situation by living out an injustice.

This all may seem counterintuitive to you at first. You are going to want to tell your wife she is wrong about you. You are going to want her to know the truth, but I encourage you to give this a shot. Though I'm not in a place where I always practice this perfectly, trust me; my wife can confirm. I have found that when I approach a disagreement from a place where it's my fault even though everything within me is screaming that it's not my fault, peace finds a way in. It's a peace that passes understanding. I have found that when I don't fight for what I see as justice, the Man I came face to face with in my twenties brings true justice. When I choose not to bring clarity or understanding based on my selfish wants and desires, and assume the role of the guilty like Jesus did, true justice comes.

I can tell you from experience that this was a challenging principle for me to learn to apply. I have always despised saying I'm sorry for something I didn't do. I can remember saying things like, "I will always apologize if I'm wrong, but why would I apologize if I'm not?" What I've learned is that loving my wife like Christ loves the Church is apologizing even when you don't think you're wrong. I'm not talking about a half-hearted "I'm sorry" like a child might do just to get out of a punishment and move on. I'm talking about a sincere apology—an apology that includes hugs and kisses. This is the kind of apology that takes the blame and the responsibility and is willing to do it next time, too. I am talking about an apology that convinces your wife that you are ready to shoulder the blame. Trust me, everyone knows the role they play in a disagreement. Everyone knows that it takes two to tango. When we as husbands decide that we want to love our wives like Jesus loves the Church, we choose to accept the indictment for a crime we may not have committed.

You may ask, "Paul, where is the hope in this for me? What if I spend the rest of my life just taking the blame for things, and nothing changes?" I asked God those same questions as He was revealing His heart to me concerning this matter. He gave me two answers for you. First, my prayer is that you experience what I experienced when I practiced this principle—peace in my home. I have learned that as I take the blame and apologize when I don't think I'm wrong, it has an effect on both my wife's heart and mine. As I mentioned earlier, we both know that we have a role to play, but when I take the initiative to take the blame, true justice always finds its way in. I have found that as I love my wife this way, her respect for me increases. Second, be prepared to take the blame for the rest of your days because it may never change anything. When God gave me this answer, He brought to my attention that He took the blame for all mankind, but not all of humanity responded with respect or love for Him. I don't believe this is how it will be for you, but it's not our job to change our wives; it is our calling to be transformed into the image of Jesus. If we are only doing the things in this book to gain a response, then it's not unconditional and therefore isn't the way Christ loves.

1. When I know I'm right, am I willing to take the blame to allow the justice of the kingdom to prevail? If not, what is preventing me?

2. Am I willing to step up and always accept responsibility for a disagreement even when I don't think it's my fault?

3. Will I explore ways that I could have better handled situations and apologize for them?

4. Am I willing to always apologize first? (This is an area where we as husbands need to lead by example. It may feel like injustice, and you know what, sometimes it is. That's exactly how Jesus loved us. His death wasn't just, but He did it because it's how He loved us, and it's how you are to love your wife.)

5. Am I willing to take the blame even if my wife never comes to admit her part in our disagreement?

LET'S PRAY

Heavenly Father, thank You for the amazing revelation of how taking the blame is a way I am to love my wife like You love Your Church. You know me and my inclination to claim personal justice. It's really tough for me to take the blame for something I didn't do. I am asking for Your strength to be more like You. I want to love like You, listen like You, and take the blame like You did. I'm humbled by Your offer to help me walk like You in my marriage. Help me to be more like You and to allow that to be expressed through loving my wife like You love Your Church. In Jesus' name, amen.

THOUGHTS & REFLECTIONS

CHAPTER NINE

HOLD YOUR TONGUE

LISTEN. LISTEN SOME MORE. THEN REALIZE YOU NEED TO LISTEN AGAIN.

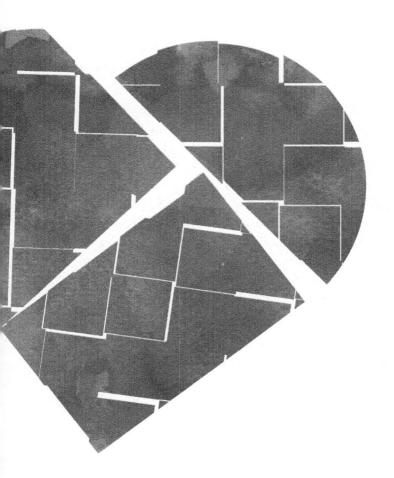

But when he was accused by the chief priests and elders,
he gave no answer. Then Pilate said to him, "Do you not
hear how many things they testify against you?" But he
gave him no answer, not even to a single charge, so that
the governor was greatly amazed.

Matthew 27:12–14

I understand that you're probably reading this without knowing me personally. But I can assure you that if you did, the one thing you would never say is, "Paul knows when to be quiet."

I have always been known for not only the rate at which I talk but also the volume. In elementary school, there was always a note on each of my grade cards that read, "Paul is a good student, but he talks too much in class." I grew to be the kind of person who thought he was usually right and wanted everyone to know that. I especially wanted you to know this if you disagreed with me. I also had a deep need to make sure I was fully and correctly understood. As an adult, this often led to debates with friends and strangers. I'm not sure if you can identify with me on this or not, but I hope I can draw an adequate picture of who I am when it comes to not holding my tongue.

I'm the kind of person who, when faced with an accusation, could always argue why you were wrong, and I was right. It was more than just a need to express my feelings. I had a deep, burning impulse to get my point across. If I felt like I was being misunderstood, it only made me argue more intently and more intensely. Holding my tongue wasn't a thing I did or a thing I was comfortable considering doing. Defending myself was what I did best. Maybe it was so important to me to defend myself because of moments I had in my younger days. Maybe moments like the accusation in the hall made me less tolerant when it came to being misunderstood. That being said, when God revealed to me that one way He modeled love for my wife through His love for the Church was through holding His tongue and not defending himself, I was floored. Let's explore my need to verbally defend myself to see how to unravel this natural, human impulse.

As I considered why I've always felt so strongly about defending myself, I thought back to high school. Something that people who do know me best will find hard to believe is that when I was a freshman in high school, I was bullied. I was the new kid in a town where I didn't know anyone. It was a whole new world for me, and for some reason, there was a group of kids who decided that they were going to make my life a living hell. I didn't know them, and they didn't know me, but for some reason, they chose me to be the one they would attack. I never knew which direction they would come from. I might get shoved against a wall one day, have my food tray knocked out of my hands another, or even better, I might take a snowball to the face on a cold winter day. To make matters worse, I didn't have any friends to defend me. I hadn't been in town long enough to connect with anyone. I was left to deal with this on my own.

Leaving the town I grew up in meant leaving all the family and friends that would have defended me. They would never have let this happen. They would have supported me and at least cheered me on as I defended myself against my attackers. But in this new environment, I had no friends and was completely exposed to the attacks of my new enemies. My dad taught me,

"Never start a fight, but always be willing to finish it." Yet for some reason, I felt so weak and insecure that year. I couldn't defend myself, and there was no one else there to protect me.

As I think about the fifteen-year-old version of me, I find myself considering how different the man I am is from that boy. I think about all the things that happened that made me who I am today. Remembering that misunderstood and bullied young man of fifteen led me to ponder the time Jesus didn't defend himself. He let his accusers attack Him with no response. As He entered the city, he was greeted by crowds of people, all excited to get a glimpse of Him. The streets were filled with friends and family celebrating His arrival. What was going through His mind? Did He know that in less than a week, He would be standing before Pontius Pilate, and most of His friends and family would be nowhere in sight? He would stand before His accuser with no one there to stand up for Him. There was no one to defend Him. I wonder if at that moment He felt the way I did at fifteen. I wonder if deep down inside, He wanted to scream out, "Injustice! I didn't do this. I'm not who you think I am!" I wonder if He felt as alone as I did when I was new to town with no friends to stand up for me. I wonder what Jesus was thinking when Pilate read the list of things he had been accused of while holding His tongue.

Fast-forward to His punishment. His choice not to defend himself led Jesus to be beaten, horribly beaten, before He went to be crucified for crimes He didn't commit. It's difficult to understand a love so great that He would say nothing and just do what the Father said to do. He truly had given up His will. I know me, and I know what I would want to do if I was standing in front of Pilate as he read the charges. I would want to say, "Wait; that's not the whole story. I'm not the guilty one!" I would fight with everything within me to keep from taking the punishment. I would want to defend myself, but because of His love for the Church, He didn't. Jesus held His tongue. He was more like the fifteen-year-old version of me: No friends. All bullies.

I imagine Jesus on the Cross. He is about to give His life in exchange for mine. The humanity of Jesus must have questioned it all. Yes, He had given up His will. Yes, He had taken the blame, but now He couldn't defend himself. My dad said, "Never start a fight, but always be willing to finish it." The Father was saying the same but from a completely different angle. I always understood this to mean never to throw the first punch, but never let them beat you up. But as God the Father said to His Son, He had a different plan for finishing. We would overcome by the blood shed by His Son. We would overcome by the word of our testimony. As Jesus took the punishment for his Bride, I like to imagine he foresaw all the testimonies that would rise because of His sacrifice. I hope He heard all that we would say because of His silence. At that moment, that moment when He felt that even His Father had forsaken Him, I imagine Him thinking, *we don't start fights*, just before He said, "It is finished" (John 19:30).

Now I feel like I have a pretty good understanding of how Jesus loved the Church by holding his tongue. So, how am I ever going to apply this to my marriage, to my love for my wife? If I'm to be honest here, this has been the hardest principle for me to apply. I can assure you that loving like Jesus isn't easy. It takes more than a mental awareness of an idea. It takes asking for His heart. I have asked God many times to help me hold my tongue, but more often than not, I chose my will over His and failed at it.

We all have certain expectations when it comes to what we want as a husband. If our wives misinterpret our motivations, we typically react by defending ourselves. When our wives tell us what we are thinking about a specific topic, but they have misunderstood our motives, we want to set their thinking straight. When has that ever worked out well for you? Maybe you are better at articulating your feelings than I am. I can tell you from my experience that there hasn't been a time when I stood up to defend myself, and it worked out well. I've never shouted, "Injustice! I didn't do this. I'm not who you think I am!" to the things my wife said, and it ended with her saying, "Oh Paul, you are right. I just misunderstood."

In reality, not all the negativity that comes through your wife is even coming from her. There are times when your wife will say something that hurts, and it's entirely an attack from the enemy. The enemy will use those closest to us to distract and destroy us. Instead of praying that God change our wives, we should be praying that God would shield us and our minds from the attacks of the enemy. We are one with our wives, so if he attacks her, he attacks us. And it's not only your wife that is susceptible to speak words that are straight from the enemy. Let Ephesians 2:29 guide what you say: "Let no corrupting talk come out of your mouths, but only such as is good for building up, as fits the occasion, that it may give grace to those who hear." And if you don't have things to say like that, muster the strength of silence.

I have learned that silence is power, and it takes strength to be silent. It takes a strength that doesn't come from your humanity, but from God's Spirit living inside of you. Jesus gave up His will, took the blame, and was quiet about it. Because of that, all believers have the Holy Spirit living in them to give strength in these tough moments. We don't have to be that fifteen-year-old with no friends. We now have "a friend who sticks closer than a brother" (Proverbs 18:24). We are no longer powerless against the attacks. I want to encourage you in this. I promise you, practicing this principle will be the hardest thing you will do. I also guarantee you that there is nothing more rewarding than successfully holding your tongue and seeing how it brings peace to the situation. You also get to avoid the chance of actually saying something stupid and only making things worse. That's what I usually do. One scripture that summarizes this for me is James 1:19, which says, "Know this, my beloved brothers: let every person be quick to hear, slow to speak, slow to anger."

Actually, if you want a quick lesson on how not holding the tongue can harm a situation, read the entire book of James. I want to share one more scripture from there. James 3:5–6 says, "So also the tongue is a small member, yet it boasts of great things. How great a forest is set ablaze by such a small fire! And the tongue is a fire, a world of unrighteousness. The tongue is set among our members, staining the whole body, setting on fire the entire course of life, and set on fire by hell."

The very powers to bring life or death into your family are held in your tongue. You can kill or bring life, all with the words you choose. Yes, it's hard to stay silent in the face of what we see as injustice. It's hard not to defend ourselves when we know that the things that are being said are inaccurate. When I start getting frustrated and desire to defend myself, the Holy Spirit often reminds me of Exodus 14:14 that says, "The Lord will fight for you, and you have only to be silent."

As I began to learn the principles of holding my tongue and not defending myself, God wasn't just teaching me how to be a better husband. He was developing me into a person who was more like Him. Life is full of moments when I want to defend myself, whether it's at home, work, or even at church. I want to defend my reputation. But the Holy Spirit softly whispers, "Hold your tongue." It's not easy. But every time I do, He proves Exodus 14:14 to be true. Whether it was a matter of being misunderstood or a situation where someone was flat-out making up stories about me, if I held my tongue and stood still, He fought my battle every time. He has proved it over and over. Yet for some reason, it is difficult for me to practice this in my marriage. There is something challenging about coming to a place of submission to God when it comes to my relationship with my wife. Yet it's what Jesus did for His Bride, and it's something He has instructed us to do as we love our wives.

ASK YOURSELF

1. Am I willing to hold my tongue when having a disagreement with my wife, even if I'm right?

2. How do I identify the moment that a discussion with my wife becomes a disagreement when I need to be silent?

3. Am I willing to find a way only to speak life to my wife? (As you speak life and avoid speaking death, you will begin to see your relationship with your wife flourish.)

4. Am I willing to let the Lord fight my battles to bring peace and justice to every situation instead of taking what I consider to be justice in my own hands?

LET'S PRAY

Heavenly Father, help me not to become discouraged or frustrated when my wife says or does things that would typically affect me emotionally. Give me the strength to hold my tongue, stand still, and allow You to fight my battles by doing Your work in my marriage. Give me the strength and wisdom to be a peacemaker, no matter how hard it is. I pray that the fruit of the Spirit in my life will be evident to my wife. This week, I will hold my tongue. I also ask that You would encourage my heart so that I don't get upset so quickly. I pray that Your Spirit will remind me to be calm and not respond hastily. I ask that You help me to give my wife the love and grace that You have extended to me. In Jesus' name, amen.

THOUGHTS & REFLECTIONS

CHAPTER TEN

BEAR THE BURDEN

LEARNING HOW TO CARRY HER ON YOUR SHOULDERS

Blessed be the Lord, who daily bears us up;
God is our salvation.

Psalms 68:19

As I pondered precisely what bearing my wife's burden looked like, I felt like I needed clarity on how Jesus bore mine. I know that may seem self-explanatory, but one thing I can say that I have learned through the process of writing this book is that God's truth is often deeper than it seems. Words have multiple meanings, and there numerous things to learn when the Lord is speaking. I think it's easiest for me to understand when put in the context of Revelation 14:2 that says, "And I heard a voice from heaven like the roar of many waters and like the sound of loud thunder. The voice I heard was like the sound of harpists playing on their harps." In my personal experience, I have found this to mean that God often says one thing, but it has many meanings. His voice is like many waters. It flows in every direction, but it always leads back to the ocean of His love.

What is God saying about bearing my burden and how that should translate to my bearing my wife's burden? As I considered and sought the Lord for an answer, I began to recognize that there are many roles that God plays in our lives: Father, Friend, Husband, Lover, Brother, etc. Each of these descriptions of our relationship with Him takes on a specific manifestation in our lives. We most often think of Him as Father, and naturally, if we didn't have an excellent relationship with our earthly dad, we may see God through that filter. I can assure you that no matter how good your human dad was, your heavenly Father is better. He is more in love with you and more interested in the dreams He has for you than your earthly dad could be. Though this is a book about being a better husband, I feel this chapter leading me to talk about the ways He bears our burdens. That requires me to talk about the different roles that God plays in our lives.

How does God bear our burdens? The Bible is a good source for this answer. It's a love letter that shows us what He did to be in a relationship with us. It's also an instruction manual on how to pursue a relationship with Him. It's a story of the God who wanted to be in a relationship with His creation. He is the God who would give anything to restore the relationship that we destroyed. He gave His very life to restore that relationship. 1 Peter 2:24 says, "He himself bore our sins in his body on the tree, that we might die to sin and live to righteousness. By his wounds you have been healed."

God bore the burden of our sin on the Cross. It seemed a little challenging to leap from such a heavy action to apply it to living as a good husband. I then was reminded that He wants to carry my cares and concerns. 1 Peter 5:6–7 says, "Humble yourselves, therefore, under the mighty hand of God so that at the proper time he may exalt you, casting all your anxieties on Him, because he cares for you." I began to meditate on those two scriptures. He bore my sins so I could live. He took all my worries because He cares about me. He bore my sin and worry because He cares about me. One of the ways He loves me is that He took care of the things that I worry about because he cares about me and my quality of life. I love how John 10:10 puts it: "The thief comes only to steal and kill and destroy. I came that they may have life and have it abundantly."

He bears my burden, so I don't need to worry; I can have

a rich and satisfying life. Got it. Now that I have at least what I think is a working understanding of how He bears my burden, I asked Him how I could apply that to how I love my wife. The whole purpose of this journey was to understand the way Christ loves the Church and then apply that principle to my life. I spent some real time here, trying to comprehend how to bear my wife's burden. Then I felt God ask me a simple question, "What is she so worried about that would keep her from having a rich and satisfying life?" My mind quickly began to compile a list of things that I had heard my wife share with me that brought her stress or worry. At that point in my life, my wife handled the finances. She was in charge of making sure all of our bills were paid, with money left over for groceries, clothes, and all of the other necessities. I had never done this before and was terrible managing my money before I was married, but I took a chance. I told her that I would start managing the money and take that off of her plate. I have now been managing our finances, with much success I might add, for the past ten years. This might seem like a little thing to you. Maybe you already manage your finances, but honestly, the point is less about the examples I share and more about you, as a husband, identifying what it is that is robbing your wife of a rich and satisfying life. It may not be fun for you, and it may not be something you really want to do, but just like 1 Peter 2:24 explains, "by his wounds you have been healed." By your wounds, if we can actually stretch it that far, your wife is healed. As you take her place on her cross, she receives life.

So let me talk about a few other areas I recognized where my wife needed me to bear her burden. I already talked about the revelation regarding folding laundry, but honestly, that wasn't a big deal to her. That was just one little thing that I could do to take things off of her mind so she could focus on the areas where God was calling her. I think we don't realize all of the things that get in the way of the dreams that God has put in our hearts, especially when it comes to our wives. Women, at least from what I can tell, have a deep desire to build a home and grow a family. They put a lot of pressure on themselves to be the perfect mom, the perfect wife, and the perfect woman. In everything they do, they feel pressure to do it to the best of their abilities. Often they are left feeling like a failure because, in their eyes, someone is doing it better than them.

We, as men, get so caught up in our work and our hobbies that we forget that there is a lot of stuff happening behind the scenes while we are absent from the home. Some of us create a self-importance that makes us feel as though we don't have time to deal with all of the inside-of-the-home stuff like bills, laundry, dishes, meal prep, helping kids with homework, sending thank you cards, cleaning toilets, sweeping and mopping floors, scrubbing bathtubs, and cooking meals. Do you get the picture? Again, I don't want you to fully make this about the tasks that I have taken off my wife's plate. This is about your identifying what is stealing your wife's joy and then sacrificing yourself for it. Die to yourself so she might have a rich and satisfying life.

You may be asking, how do I figure out what I need to do for my wife? Here are a couple of tips:

1. Listen to her. Husbands often don't stop and actually listen to the concerns our wives are voicing. We discount them as complaining, and in our minds, we have plenty to worry about. So, we ignore what they are saying about what is bothering them. I suggest that you make a concerted effort to listen to your wife and hear what she has to say. She will let you know where you can help.

2. Ask her. This can be scary because we might not really want to know what our wives wants us to take off their plates. Nonetheless, I'm telling you right now to do it! It will change your life, and it will change your marriage. Ask her today, "What can I do to help bear your burden? If there was one thing that you do around here that you wish you didn't have to do, what would it be?" I can assure you that your wife will have an answer, and the next step is for you to start doing it.

I can speak from experience that if you start practicing this principle, you will get tired of always separating the laundry, washing the laundry, drying the laundry, and folding the laundry. You will get tired of always making sure the carpet is vacuumed. You will begin to tire of pulling weeds, paying bills, buying groceries, cooking meals, and emptying the dishwasher. It's in those moments that you start to feel the pain of bearing your wife's burden. And no matter what has you exhausted, I want you to remember the Cross and the way that Jesus loved you, the way He loved the Church. He bore our pain so we can have rich and satisfying lives. While you do the things that she doesn't want to do, send her outside to enjoy a nice, cold beverage in the hammock. That is the moment you really start loving your wife like Christ loves the Church.

I need to add a little warning here. Some of these things you will have zero problem doing. They may even make you happy that you're helping. But over time, as you continue to take everything she wants to let go, you will tire. Keep this in mind—Jesus didn't bear just part of our sin. He didn't take only a few of our burdens; He took them all. He was worn out, beat up, tired, maybe even a little frustrated, but He did it anyway. As you start practicing this principle, you may be exhausted, but you will also begin to see a shift in your marriage. Your wife will notice the change in you. She might not always tell you, and she might even get so used to you doing this that she doesn't even notice, but keep on doing it.

Remember, Jesus did all these things for a Bride that often neglects Him, that often forgets Him, and that often forgets precisely what He did for Her. Yet He still did it.

I have found that the enemy will try to convince you that your wife is taking you for granted, as you try to serve more. He will tell you that you deserve better and that she doesn't appreciate you. The enemy is a liar and is trying to kill, steal, and destroy. Service is love, and love is service. It's a never-ending circle of the heart of the Father. I have found that the tighter I embraced this principle, the easier it has been for me to put it into practice. This may not be true for you. Maybe holding your tongue is more natural, or perhaps giving up your will is easiest. But it's not just one of these that He did. He loved the Church by doing all of this, and all of these are ways you can love your wife. I have found that as I take things off of my wife's plate, I want to do more. I have now come to a place where I do things that I know are on her list just so that they aren't on her list anymore. There is very little that brings me more joy than to have her cup of coffee waiting for her when she gets out of the shower in the morning. I love to have her breakfast made when she walks into the kitchen. I love to complete things she needs to get done without her even knowing I'm doing it.

Maybe you're thinking, *I'm busy with my own stuff. I don't have time to do this.* I want to encourage you by letting you know that even now, I work a full-time job that requires travel and about 60 hours a week of my time. Yet, I have found a way to sacrifice myself so that she can have a rich and satisfying life. I'm not bragging. I'm not superhuman. Actually, I'm very human. I screw up every day. I make many mistakes. I just want to testify to you that if I can do it, you can do it! I am determined to be Jesus to my wife because He first loved me. Our goal is to have great marriages. We want our wives to love and respect us. If we really want this, we need to take the first step. 1 John 4:19 says, "We love because he first loved us." We didn't love Him first. We love Him because He showed the first love. The same applies to our marriages. If we want our wives to love us the way we need to be loved, it's on us to love them first. So start showing her your love today by bearing her burden. You can do it!

1. Am I doing all I can to free my wife up so she can pursue the dreams God has placed in her heart? If not, list a few ways you can start freeing up some of her time.

2. Am I willing to take things off of my wife's plate that may make me uncomfortable to help her have a richer and more satisfying life?

3. Am I more concerned about my schedule and my time than I am about giving my wife more freedom in her schedule? (If you don't know your wife's schedule, make time to talk to her about everything she has going on.)

LET'S PRAY

Heavenly Father, You are so good. Thank You for loving me so much that You bore the burden of my sin so that I can have a rich and satisfying life. You are so good to me, and I want to be that good to my wife. Help me to love my wife like You love Your Bride. Help me to help her in areas that are stealing her joy and keeping her from the satisfying life she could have. You have created her with purpose and have called me to support and empower her. Please provide me with wisdom to understand how I can help her follow the dreams that You placed in her heart. Give me the strength to bear not only my burdens, but also her burdens. Help me to be a cheerful giver when it comes to serving my wife like You served Your Church. In Jesus' name, amen.

THOUGHTS & REFLECTIONS

CHAPTER ELEVEN

TAKE ME, NOT HER

DEVELOPING SACRIFICIAL LOVE WITHOUT EXPECTATIONS.

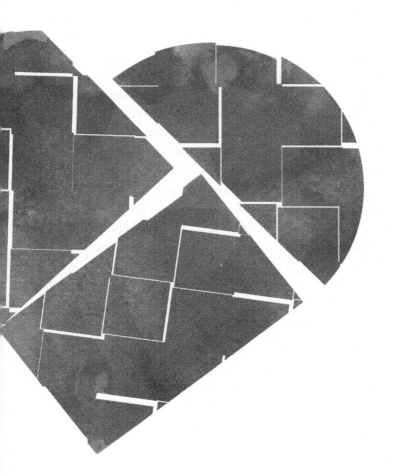

Husbands, love your wives, as Christ loved the church and gave himself up for her.

Ephesians 5:25

A s I worked through the ideas behind this book, I tried to sit down and consider precisely what Jesus was feeling and thinking when He set the example for me loving my wife. As I consider this chapter, Take Me, Not Her, I am allowing myself to see Him on that day, that day that He made the ultimate sacrifice for His Bride. It was the most self-less act of love. I imagine Him having gone through the journey from the Garden to the grave. He came to terms with giving up His will, and that decision determined the rest of His actions over the next couple of days. He gave up His will. He held His tongue. He took the blame. He bore the burden. Finally, he died. When we consider dying for our wives, I'm sure that the majority of us would quickly respond, "Take me, not her" in a tragic situation. Most of us would walk on the side of the sidewalk closest to the street. Most of us would jump in front of a bullet to save our bride. That's exactly what Jesus did. He went through the pain and suffering so His Bride wouldn't have to. The mocking was for us. The beating was for us. The death penalty was for us. But in action, He said, "take me, not her."

When I allow myself to consider what happened on the Cross, it's crazy to me. Jesus was in love with a Bride who wasn't fit to be married to a King, *the* King. He had a love for a girl who was from the proverbial other side of town. He was rich; She was poor. He was royalty; She was a pauper. His robe was clean and spotless, and She was dirty from head to toe. It sounds no different than any other story of forbidden love, but in this case, his Father didn't forbid. His Father encouraged the relationship. Ephesians 5:25–27 says, "Husbands, love your wives, as Christ loved the church and gave himself up for her, that he might sanctify her, having cleansed her by the washing of water with the word, so that he might present the church to himself in splendor, without spot or wrinkle or any such thing, that she might be holy and without blemish."

He gave up His life for the sake of His Bride's holiness and cleanliness. He did this so His Bride would be like Him. His relationship with us was more important than His own life. By giving up His life, His Bride could live Her life as the purposed and called Bride She became through His death. He saw Her potential past the ugliness and the dirtiness. He saw who She would be after She was cleansed as a result of His sacrifice. In His act of selflessness, His Bride moved from a pauper to a princess and realized Her full potential. In finding herself, she also discovered Her love for Him.

Though we have established that most of us would give up our literal lives for our wives, I think we are being asked to look at this a little more deeply. He gave up His life to make her holy and clean, washed by the cleansing of God's Word. This makes me ask myself, *When was the last time I washed my wife with God's Word? What does that even mean? What does that look like?* I think it looks like giving up my will. It must look like praying for her. It must look like taking the blame. It must look like holding my tongue. It must look like bearing her burden. It must look like dying to myself, and in the process of loving her like Jesus, she becomes the wife she has been called to be. As I die to me, she lives as her. As I live out the love that Jesus has for his Bride, my wife becomes the person she was created to be. She begins to become the wife that she is called to be.

We will never be able to demand that our wives love us the way we want to be loved. We will never be able to insist that they respect us the way we need to be respected. We can only control what we can control, and that is what Jesus did. He didn't and doesn't demand that we love Him the way He wants to be loved. Jesus doesn't insist that we give Him the respect He is due. He controlled what he could control, and he absolutely gave up everything to have the girl of his dreams.

I have watched this principle come alive in my personal life. For so long, I wanted my wife to be a certain way. I wanted her to speak my love language and to make me feel the way I thought I wanted or even needed to feel. All of my actions were driven by the selfish motivation of my personal wants and needs. I rubbed her feet because I wanted sex. I made her dinner because I wanted to watch the game with the guys. I washed the dishes because I wanted her respect. Through all of the sacrifices I made, my motivation had very little to do with serving my wife. Almost everything to do with what I hoped to get out of it.

As I compare my selfish actions to the example Jesus set, I see such a contrast between the two. While I became frustrated because my actions didn't earn the love and respect that I wanted, Jesus was softly reminding me that He did everything with no expectation of anything in return. He didn't die to manipulate us into responding how He wanted. He died for us in hopes that we would choose to be in a relationship with Him. While I spent time rejecting my wife because she didn't act the way I thought she should, Jesus modeled dying to His wants and His needs to show me the better way. He completely died to himself in spite of my failure to love Him the way He desires. He died with the hope that I would respond to His sacrifice with an openness to love Him the way He desires. His wants and desires are not much different than many of ours; He desires a close relationship with us. He desires to be respected. He desires conversations. He desires to be understood. Though He holds many of the same relationship goals for us, He would die over and over again to give us the opportunity to be in a relationship with Him, even if we never choose to. That is unconditional love.

1. Do I need my wife to give me all I want to feel like she loves me? Does she have to earn my love, or is my love unconditional?

2. Do I offer selfish acts of service to my wife to try and solicit a response from her? How could I selflessly do those same acts?

3. Am I willing to sacrifice my wants and needs in an honest pursuit of a deep relationship with my wife?

LET'S PRAY

Heavenly Father, thank You for wanting to be in a relationship with me. I'm sorry for the times I forget all You did to pursue me. I'm so thankful that You desire time with me. Help me to be like You and love like You when it comes to my wife. Help me to love unconditionally. Help me to be willing to die to myself so that she can live. I want a full and deep relationship with her, and I can see that following Your example is the first step in making that happen. Help me not to be discouraged if I don't immediately see the response that I hope for. Please give me strength to continue down the path You set me on to be the husband I'm called to be. In Jesus' name, amen.

THOUGHTS & REFLECTIONS

CHAPTER TWELVE

FIGHT LIKE A MAN

BE WHO YOU WERE
CREATED TO BE.

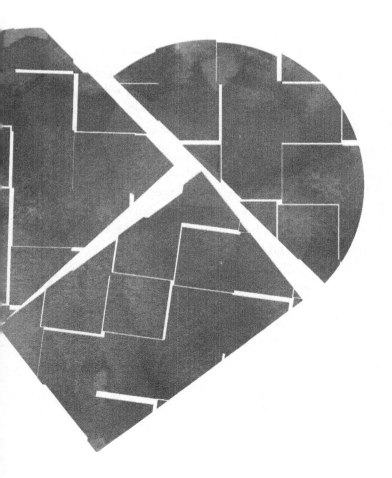

Iron sharpens iron, and one man sharpens another.

Proverbs 27:17

S o here we sit with a lot of things to consider. There have been many challenges set before us. Trust me; I know this isn't easy. For over ten years, I have put these principles into practice and still fail daily. As I try to live out all that has been revealed to me, I am reminded of Luke 9:23, where Jesus said, "If anyone would come after me, let him deny himself and take up his cross daily and follow me." Marriage is a daily journey. A successful, godly marriage starts with taking up your cross daily. A great marriage isn't something that will happen overnight. This isn't a get-rich-quick scheme or a fad diet; this is hard work. The principles in this book are a challenging but effective way.

As I've shared these principles with others, some have embraced the ideas, and some have rejected them. I am aware that it all sounds impossible to some. I am also mindful that it all seems too good to be true for others. Honestly, I get it. I have failed so much at this that I'm probably failing at it in some way even as you're reading this. Thankfully, my failures don't have to determine your outcomes. Both of us have to daily decide if we will be like Jesus in our homes. Are we going to love our wives as Christ loves the Church? If we agree that He did all of the things mentioned earlier because He loved the Church, then it only comes down to whether we are going to love our wives that way or not.

As we consider just how difficult the work is, let me share with you one last moment from my childhood. Back when I was a kid, it was before all of the anti-bullying campaigns that we have today. When confronted by a bully, it was assumed that there were two options:

1. Run away.
2. Fight back.

My Dad always taught me to fight for what I believed in. He always taught me to stand up for myself and instilled this idea of standing up and fighting like a man. Of course, this isn't intended as an insult to women (my experience is that women are actually the toughest of our species). But as a man, even as a kid, I was taught to fight like a man. What does that mean? What it meant to me was this: stand up for what you believe in. Don't let others destroy or belittle what matters to you. Defend the innocent. Defend my family. Don't shrink before a challenge; stand up and fight like a man. As I consider this idea, I am humbled to realize that I have been given something that must be defended. I have been given something that must be stood up for. I have been given a marriage to my wife that represents our relationship with God. What could be more valuable, as a husband, to stand up and fight for?

Over the time I've worked on this book, I've had the opportunity to visit with many men. I have enjoyed becoming part of their respective journeys. As I spent time discussing these matters, they all made it clear that if they could share one thing, it would be the following: as you begin practicing these principles, it's going to get harder before it gets better. I will absolutely agree with this.

I can promise you that there will be many failures and disappointments. There will be times you feel your marriage is only getting worse. There will be times you will question whether you have the strength to love the way Jesus loves. The last thing the enemy wants is for you to begin to love like Jesus. Ever since Adam and Eve, the enemy's intention was to cause division between the couple. But Jesus has given us the perfect example. There is a reason that the Church is referred to as the Bride of Christ. There is a reason that Paul wrote that husbands should model their love for their wives on Christ's love for the Church. Our relationships with our wives is to be modeled after our relationship with Jesus. He showed us how to be a great husband through His actions.

As our love becomes increasingly unconditional, and as we learn to give up our pride and our will, we begin to spread the love of God in our homes and our world. Things will get harder before they get better because this is war against darkness. Division and divorce are tools that the enemy uses to separate us from each other and to make us feel like we are separated from God. There are moments when I all but give up. But God's Spirit reminds me that I'm not doing this to gain a response from my wife. I'm not dying for her to gain something from her. I'm dying for her to create an opportunity for a relationship. I want our relationship to be based on a Jesus-like love—an unconditional love. I'm not giving up my will in hopes that my wife will give up hers. I'm giving up my will because I want to be like Jesus. I want to encourage you with Romans 8:31–39:

> What then shall we say to these things? If God is for us, who can be against us? He who did not spare his own Son but gave him up for us all, how will he not also with him graciously give us all things? Who shall bring any charge against God's elect? It is God who justifies. Who is to condemn? Christ Jesus is the one who died—more than that, who was raised—who is at the right hand of God, who indeed is interceding for us. Who shall

separate us from the love of Christ? Shall tribulation, or distress, or persecution, or famine, or nakedness, or danger, or sword? As it is written,

> "For your sake we are being killed all the day long; we are regarded as sheep to be slaughtered."

No, in all these things we are more than conquerors through him who loved us. For I am sure that neither death nor life, nor angels nor rulers, nor things present nor things to come, nor powers, nor height nor depth, nor anything else in all creation, will be able to separate us from the love of God in Christ Jesus our Lord.

As I read this passage from Romans, I began to ask myself if my wife could insert my name in the passage. I'm not saying that we're actually Jesus or a replacement of Him. I mean it in the sense that we are called to love like Him, and I wonder if this passage would be true for my wife if my name were in there. So, let's do it for fun. I'll use me as the example but you should use your own name. If my wife was reciting Romans 8 about her marriage, could she say:

If Paul is for me, who can be against me?

Paul would die for me.

Paul is pleading to God for me.

I am convinced that nothing can separate me from the love of Paul.

This may be a little awkward for you; it was for me. The point is that if this passage demonstrates how we are supposed to love our wives, then it is a useful metric to see how we measure up.

I'm not one to give guarantees. Honestly, I can't promise that if you practice the principles of this book that you will have the perfect marriage you always wanted with your wife. There is one guarantee that I can make: If you correctly practice these principles, Jesus will have the marriage He always wanted with you. As you become more like Him, you become the pure bride you were meant to be.

It makes me think of something I heard once. I heard that the longer people are married, the more they begin to act and even look like each other. That is the marriage that I'm looking for when it comes to being the Bride of Christ. The more we practice being like Him, the more we begin to look like Him. The more we look like Him, the more people will know we are married to Him. As our wives see us respond like Jesus to them, they will see Jesus in us, and they will desire to be closer to us.

I know I already told you that it's not easy. I told you that the enemy would attack your marriage when you declare war by working to be more like Jesus. Now I want to encourage you through the process of trying to be a husband that loves his wife as Christ loves the Church. It won't always be easy, but it will get easier. As you spend time trying to be more like Jesus, you will become more like Jesus. As you spend time trying to love more unconditionally, you will love more unconditionally. As you begin to take the blame, it will hurt your pride less. As you spend more time taking the blame, you will care less about your perceived notions of what justice is. You will have moments when your flesh will rise up, but as you invite the Holy Spirit to come, you will feel the love, joy, and peace that shows up with that prayer.

I will leave you with this story in hopes that it will encourage you As I was writing this book, I had set a loose deadline for completion, and it was the day before that date. I still had two chapters to write, and I thought I would spend time writing those chapters later in the day. I spent the morning with my family, but I was really on edge for some reason. I was impatient. I was unreasonable. I was not practicing the principles of this book. We finally got home, and honestly, I don't think anyone wanted to be around me, especially my wife. She knew that I planned on working on the book and strongly encouraged me to go because I was so hard to be around.

The way that I acted left me feeling separated from my wife. As you probably already expect, the last thing I felt like doing was writing two chapters on loving my wife like Christ loves the Church. I felt like a bad husband. I felt like a bad dad. Instead of writing, I just went to my office and sat and prayed. I told God how I couldn't do it, how I couldn't love like Him. About that time, a buddy of mine who has been a big part of the book process texted me and asked how things were going with the book. I told him exactly where I was. I told him that I was having trouble because of the way things had gone between my wife and me that day. He responded with three words: "Holy Spirit, come." He used my own words on me. Right then and there, I began to ask the Holy Spirit to come. At that moment, I felt His peace. I felt the Spirit of reconciliation come over me.

I reached out to my wife and took the blame for everything. In this particular case, it was all my blame to take anyway. I guess I tell you this because I want you to know that even while I was writing this, I struggled. Even while writing this book, I needed someone to remind me of what the book said. I also want to tell you that it worked. When I invited the Holy Spirit to join me where I was, He did. He brought peace, humility, and comfort. As you pursue loving Your bride like He loves His Bride, I pray that the Holy Spirit is with you the same way throughout every step of this endeavor.

ASK YOURSELF

1. Am I ready to try to practice the principles of this book? If not, what is stopping me? How does that thing measure up against the value of my marriage?

2. When facing temptation or trials in my marriage, will I invite the Holy Spirit to come?

3. Am I willing to find friends to walk with me on this journey to being the husband I am called to be? [Finding an accountability group would significantly improve your chances of success. There is power in agreement. (Matthew 18:19–20)]

LET'S PRAY

Heavenly Father, thank You for all You are doing in us. Thank You for all You are doing in our marriage with Jesus and with our wives. We ask for strength and resolve to pursue a relationship with You that influences our relationship with our wives. Help us to overcome discouragement when we fail or when things don't go the way we hoped. When we fail, I ask that you remind us to invite Your Holy Spirit to come, and He will. You will meet us where we are, and You will bring the fruit that comes with Your Spirit. We love You and thank You for our wives. Surround us with men that will encourage us in this journey of being great husbands like You. In Jesus' name, amen.

THOUGHTS & REFLECTIONS

MY PRAYER FOR YOU

To conclude the book, I'd like to let you know my prayer for you. My hope is that the words you've read challenge you to make changes that will positively affect your marriage. But hope alone isn't enough. I also have faith that as you are guided by love for God and your wife, He will make this prayer become reality.

Heavenly Father, thank You for who You are and the miracle You performed and continue in my marriage. You truly made the deaf to hear and the blind to see. You took what was dead and breathed life into it. I pray that You would do the same for the man reading this book. I ask that you would breathe Your life into what may seem dead. Remind his heart that what we call dead may only be sleeping. Awaken a passion for a relationship with You. Then awaken a passion for his spouse. I pray that what You inspired me to write finds its way deep into his heart so that it can take root and eventually produce fruit.

I ask that You lead this reader on a journey to be more like You in his home. Walk with him as he pursues a marriage that looks more like Your love for us. I ask that you soften and even turn the heart of his wife toward him as he pursues You. Please open the doors of communication in this couple. I ask that his wife would see the change that You are making in him. As he pursues your heart for marriage, protect his family from the attacks and lies of the enemy. Give them wisdom to discern between Your truth and the enemy's lies. In the moments that they are discouraged, I ask that they look to You for hope. You are our hope.

God, thank you for all You are already doing in this reader's life. Please continue that work. Thank You for modeling what a great husband looks like and helping me to be a part of showing that to him. I pray that he says what he hears You say and does what he has seen You do. In Jesus' name, amen.

HEART OF A HUSBAND